HET CHRISTELIJK HUISGEZIN # THE CHRISTIAN FAMILY

TRANSLATED BY
Nelson D. Kloosterman

HET CHRISTELIJK HUISGEZIN # THE CHRISTIAN FAMILY

TRANSLATED BY
Nelson D. Kloosterman

HERMAN BAVINCK

EDITED BY STEPHEN J. GRABILL
INTRODUCTION BY JAMES EGLINTON

GRAND RAPIDS · MICHIGAN

Copyright © 2012 by Nelson D. Kloosterman

All rights reserved. No portion of this book may be reproduced, stored in a retrieval system, or transmitted in any form or by any means electronic, mechanical, photocopy, recording, scanning, or otherwise, except for brief quotations in critical reviews or articles, without the prior written permission of the publisher.

Originally published as *Het Christelijk Huisgezin*. 2nd revised ed.
© Kampen: J. H. Kok, 1912
First published in 1908

Unless otherwise indicated, all Scripture quotations are from The Holy Bible, English Standard Version® (ESV®), copyright © 2001 by Crossway, a publishing ministry of Good News Publishers. Used by permission. All rights reserved.

ISBN 978-1-938948-14-5

Christian's Library Press
An imprint of the Acton Institute for the Study of Religion & Liberty
98 E. Fulton Street
Grand Rapids, Michigan 49503
www.clpress.com

Cover and interior design by Sharon VanLoozenoord
Editing by Stephen J. Grabill, Dylan Pahman, Timothy J. Beals, and Paul J. Brinkerhoff

21 20 19 18   2 3 4 5 6 7 8 9 10
Printed in the United States of America

CONTENTS

INTRODUCTION BY JAMES EGLINTON, *vii*

PREFACE TO THE SECOND EDITION, *xvii*

1
THE ORIGIN OF THE FAMILY, *1*

2
THE DISRUPTION OF THE FAMILY, *9*

3
THE FAMILY AMONG THE NATIONS, *15*

4
THE FAMILY IN ISRAEL, *29*

5
THE FAMILY IN THE NEW TESTAMENT, *37*

6
DANGERS CONFRONTING THE FAMILY, *51*

7
MARRIAGE AND FAMILY, *63*

8
FAMILY AND NURTURE, *87*

9
FAMILY AND SOCIETY, *109*

10
THE FUTURE OF THE FAMILY, *135*

ABOUT THE CONTRIBUTORS, *163*

SCRIPTURE INDEX, *165*

INTRODUCTION

The Christian Family in the Twenty-First Century

James Eglinton

The briefest glance at the shelves of the local Christian bookstore soon makes plain that books on the Christian family and marriage are not in short supply. Indeed, an awareness of just how many books have been written on this topic surely prompts the question as to why *this* book is worthy of translation and release in the English-speaking world. Further to that, this book was written in the early twentieth century Netherlands—a social context far removed from that of those likely to read this edition. What could Herman Bavinck's *The Christian Family* have to say to us?

In the context of mainstream evangelicalism, we are not short of moralistic "ten-step guides" aimed at building better marriages, or promise-based programs designed to create better spouses and parent-child relationships. Thanks to the influence of Mark Driscoll on evangelical attitudes towards marriage, the more recent trend has been to shift the focus towards sex, albeit still in the form of fairly crude "how to" guides. To a cynical eye, this shift looks like the evangelical subculture aping its secular host-culture's views on sex and relationships (the center of which being its uncritical adoption of secular society's assumption of hypersexuality as the norm for all). As such, the gospel becomes a means to what secular values on hypersexuality tell us we should all want: more and "hotter" sex. The current evangelical preoccupation with sex, and its accompanying reinvention of the celebrity pastor as a Christian sex guru, risks creating a new kind of prosperity gospel: Christianity might not make you healthy or wealthy, the idea goes, but it is the key to a far better sex life. Its gospel promises to fulfill the carnal longings of your (essentially secular) heart.

In short, current evangelical attitudes towards sex within marriage appear less and less radically different from their contemporary secular equivalents. In their spoon-fed approach to sex, both are increasingly banal and formulaic.

Viewed against this backdrop, the translation and rerelease of Bavinck's book on the Christian family suddenly seems more useful. This is no ten-step guide, nor is it a one-sided approach to marriage where everything is reduced to one's moral or sexual performance. Rather, this is the fruit of a rich Christian mind. It is a Christian *theology* of marriage and the family. This is a mature handling of the origins of marriage and family life, the effects of sin thereupon, a thoughtful appraisal of various historic Christian approaches to marriage and the family, and an attempt to apply that theology to the Christian family in Bavinck's own day.

Although this book is the product of a seminal Christian thinker, it is also a product of its time. There are various emphases that will strike its present-day readers as belonging to a culture very different to their own. There are also major current debates regarding the Christian concepts of marriage and family that receive scant or no attention in this book: the most obvious examples being homosexuality and the related issue of church and civil society disagreeing strongly on the definition of marriage. That said, this book has a great deal to offer to readers at the start of the twenty-first century.

This short opening essay will attempt to open up the book by first providing a biographical sketch of its author, following which

Introduction

some pointers will be given to explain various emphases in this work in relation to the hallmarks of Bavinck's thought.

Biographical Sketch

Born on December 13, 1854, in the Dutch town of Hoogeveen, Herman Bavinck was the son of Jan Bavinck, a Reformed pastor originally from Bentheim on the German-Dutch border, and Gesina Magdalena Bavinck (née Holland). The second of seven children, Herman was born into the conservative, separatist Christian Reformed Church. After completing his high school education, he enrolled as a student at the Theological School in Kampen. After one year, however, he made the daring decision to transfer to the aggressively modernist theological faculty at Leiden. The theology on offer at Leiden could scarcely have been more different to that of the seminary in Kampen.

Why did he make this move? Although the young Bavinck underwent something of a crisis of faith while at Leiden (from which he eventually emerged), his choice to study in Leiden should not be read as an abandonment of orthodox theology. Rather, his choice was primarily motivated by his search for a more rigorous academic training in theology than could be offered in Kampen at that time.

Between 1874 and 1880, Bavinck studied under the likes of Johannes Scholten and Abraham Kuenen—the then superstars of Dutch academic theology—at Leiden. There, he admired the scientific approach of his professors, though he often found himself in deep disagreement with their presuppositions and doctrinal conclusions. At this time, he also came under the influence of Abraham Kuyper, the rising star of a new wave of Dutch neo-Calvinism. His Christian Reformed pastor at Leiden, J. H. Donner, introduced him to Kuyper's Anti-Revolutionary Party (a Christian political movement directed against the anti-Christian influence of the French Revolution on Dutch society). At Leiden, Bavinck wrote a doctoral thesis on the ethics of the Swiss Reformer Ulrich Zwingli, following which he sought ordination in the Christian Reformed Church. In 1881 he became the pastor of the congregation in Franeker, a small town in the northern Netherlands.

One year later, Bavinck was called to teach theology at Kampen, where he taught from 1883 to 1901. There, he wrote his most important work, the *Reformed Dogmatics*: a modern classic of systematic theology. He married Johanna Adrianna Schippers in 1891. Johanna was ten years younger than Herman. Their only child, a daughter named Johanna Geziena, was born in 1894. During his time at Kampen, Bavinck and Kuyper were the key figures in the Union of the Reformed Churches in 1892. A decade after this Union, he accepted the post of theology professor at the Free University of Amsterdam.

This period in his life was marked by a broad and thorough engagement in the fields of politics (via the Anti-Revolutionary Party), philosophy, and education. In 1920, after preaching at Synod, Bavinck suffered a heart attack. From then onwards, his health began to fail. He died on July 29, 1921.

Bavinck's "Organic" Worldview

Bavinck's work is essentially one giant effort to develop a worldview centered on the Triune God: marriage and the family included. To Augustine's earlier conviction that our hearts remain restless until they find their rest in God, Bavinck adds that our minds remain unsatisfied until all our thoughts are brought back to the Trinity. The reality of God's glorious, eternal coexistence as the Father, the Son, and the Holy Spirit was both the beginning and end of Bavinck's theological enterprise. The Triune God is the single most important factor in Bavinck's thought: it is the reality by which all others are measured.

Introduction

That commitment to a worldview focused on the Triune God gives Bavinck's theology a very particular shape. It affected how Bavinck viewed everything: the universe, human society, the church, and, in this case, marriage and the family. In short, although Bavinck believed that God's triunity (that God is Three-in-One, and as such, the supreme model of unity-in-diversity) was utterly unique and could not be replicated elsewhere, he also believed that everything created by the Triune God somehow referred back to this divine unity-in-diversity. The universe is, after all, the general revelation of its Triune Creator.

So, while we can only find the Three-in-One formula in God himself, we find pointers to God's triunity everywhere: in the vast internal diversity of the nonetheless united universe, in the rich tapestry of human culture and society, in the nature of human sexual complementarity, in the life of the family (whereby different genders, personalities, family traditions, etc., somehow become a unit), and so on.

The language favored by Bavinck when writing of this God-centered unity-in-diversity is that of the "organic." The world made by the Trinity, and the image of that Trinity (the individual human being, and collectively, the human race) found therein, are best described as organisms, or as organic in their existence. (In the background to this, it is also interesting to know that Bavinck's constant drive to talk of God as the Trinity and the creation as organic stems largely from his reaction to the teaching he received at Leiden. There, Professor Scholten stressed that the world was run along rigid, fatalistic, mechanical, deterministic lines, and because of that, the idea of God as Trinity was of little importance).

From this desire to understand all of life as somehow pointing to the Triune God, then, various emphases in Bavinck's handling of marriage and the family come to the fore. His insistence that the family should function as an organic unit (rather than as an arbitrarily connected group of individuals who have few fixed connections to each other) makes sense in this light. Similarly, his understanding of every family unit as a unique combination of histories social and biological (as opposed to the idea that the family is a generic product needing no personal space or distinctive living environment) should be understood against this backdrop. His belief that child-rearing should view each child as a unique and complex organism to be *known* and *related to* (and not as a machine that can be so controlled), rather than be shaped by mechanical programming, is a similarly organic concern.

The organic ideas found throughout Bavinck's perspective on the Christian family should all be read as part of Bavinck's effort to see the world in the light of its Triune Creator. For Bavinck, an organic view of marriage and the family is a godly one.

Grace Restores Nature

Following this, readers of this book should also be aware of Bavinck's belief that grace restores nature. The basic structure of Bavinck's worldview is that the Triune God creates a good world, that creation then falls into sin, following which the Triune God redeems in grace. God's work in redemption is that of restoring things to their original (good) state: God's grace does not introduce new elements into the creation, or remove things that were originally present before the fall. Grace does not elevate nature, as though God's original work of creation was somehow insufficient and still needs improvement. Rather, it restores nature. It takes things back to how they were before sin had its awful way with the creation. Grace returns us to what God, in the prefall world, saw as "very good."

Although this point sounds slightly abstract at first, its practical consequences are considerable. In terms of our view of the world, its major implication is that the world—as God first made it—was inherently good. As this still sinless nature did not need to be later improved by grace (as is the case according to much Roman

Introduction

Catholic thought), it stands to reason that things found in that as-yet-unfallen world should be affirmed and celebrated. This is the basis by which Bavinck affirms that the physical world—as God's creation—is in essence good, rather than neutral or bad. While they are now affected by sin, things like food and drink, marriage, procreation, and human culture are not evil in and of themselves. Christianity would not have us focus on our souls whilst ignoring our bodies or the physical world around us. The "grace restores nature" idea is, at its core, an affirmation of nature. In the postfall world, grace does not remove our physicality, nor does it require us to live ascetic lives or disdain marriage. Rather, grace works to restore all of those things to their prefall beauty and holiness.

Bavinck's book recognizes that the Christian church has never gone as far as denouncing marriage outright. That said, he is critical of the Roman Catholic tradition (which rests on the belief that grace elevates, rather than simply restores, nature) in its tendency to regard married people as second-rate, in terms of holiness, to the celibate. The understanding of "grace restores nature" upon which this book is founded is crucial to Bavinck's support of marriage and celibacy as distinct callings, both of which can honor the Creator.

God's grace does not somehow elevate nature, but neither does it exist outside of and distant from our world. In restoring nature, grace makes its presence known in our midst. It confronts us with our need of redemption in grace. This is a helpful insight that gives Bavinck's handling of marriage and family life a gritty realism. Often, Bavinck writes, you—as a sinner—will be the main cross your spouse is called to bear. In this fallen world, there are no promises that marriage, for all its capacity to be beautiful and enriching, will be a lifelong series of ever increasing physical delights. In reality, a healthy marriage will probably lean more on the Sermon on the Mount than on the Song of Solomon. And in that respect, Bavinck's insights on marriage (all of which grow out of the various consequences of his "grace restores nature" insight) provide a helpful corrective to much imbalance in contemporary evangelical thinking on marriage.

The Family, the Individual, and Society

The movement within which Bavinck rose to prominence, neo-Calvinism, found much of its initial momentum as a rebellion against the influence of the French Revolution across Europe. This struggle to counter the impact of the Revolution exerts a defining influence upon much of Bavinck's thought on Christianity and culture. Many emphases in Bavinck's thought on the family should be understood within this context.

The Revolution was an attempt to cast aside all the old distinctions of class and power: *liberty, equality* and *fraternity* were the new values. Gone were concepts like monarchy, social class, and theism. The new de facto deity, reason, was set in direct opposition to divine revelation. The change attempted in Revolutionary France was highly ambitious: it was a movement of re-creation, an upheaval instigated to change every aspect of French life. The nineteenth-century Revolutionary intellectual Edgar Quinet recognized that such a sudden break with an entire social system could only happen if the preexisting sense of social interconnectedness between citizens was broken: those who have, until now, existed primarily in relationship to each other within a common culture must suddenly think of themselves primarily as individuals. Quinet recognized this as central not just to the French Revolution, but to all revolutionary movements. Thus, in order to change an entire society, all the old social connections had to disappear, and the "individual" had to take their place.

The great irony perceived by the likes of Bavinck and Kuyper was that although revolutionaries were told of their new-found individuality, in reality they became far more homogenous than in the pre-Revolutionary world. Revolutionary France was a place where all were pressured to dress and speak alike, where human

Introduction

worth did not exist beyond one's social standing (hence the drive for a homogenized society), and where institutions like Christian theism, as pro-social diversity, were seen as obstacles to those goals.

Having seen these ideals taking hold of France, Bavinck was motivated to combat their influence in Dutch culture. That context sets the scene for his thoughts on the family as a united social entity. His argument was that the family is not an arbitrary collective of individuals, who may or may not have much in common by way of belief. Rather, he argues in favor of the family as an organism made up of distinct but complementary people who together form the building blocks of society.

There are certainly aspects of Bavinck's vision of the organic family that are hard to maintain in the present day. For a large part of his political career, for example, Bavinck fought against individual suffrage and was against women having the right to vote (instead, Bavinck, typical of the Anti-Revolutionary Party, believed in suffrage being granted to fathers as the heads of families, with those families voting as units). His opinion later changed, eventually leading him to vote for individual male and female suffrage, despite being opposed to Revolutionary individualism in principle.

That Bavinck (seven years after the publication of this book) was willing to accept a greater degree of individualistic social participation is a useful reminder that this book, while helpful, is also limited in applicability to Western cultures one century later. The opposition to individualism undergirding the organic family unit ideals in this book is very strong. However, within a few short years Bavinck himself came to recognize that Western society was becoming increasingly individualistic. He saw this as inevitable, and later admitted that Scripture gives no clear guidance on whether families or individuals should enjoy voting rights.

Bavinck's own application of the core theological principles at hand changed following the publication of this book, which should serve as a useful reminder of the need for a careful contemporary reading of Bavinck's practical applications on the family. If we, as readers in a yet further removed cultural context, expect simply to maintain the entirety of Bavinck's practical guidance given a century before, we will be disappointed. Our task, as Christians in 2012, is not to maintain practices given in 1912 that Bavinck himself could no longer maintain by 1919. Indeed, those who so read the cultural applications in this book surely miss this book's significance: it is an excellent example of a thoughtful Christian attempting to understand marriage and the family in the light of Scripture and Christian tradition, and on that basis, who tries to articulate a Christian model of marriage for the Netherlands in his day. Our social contexts are different, and those striving for a Christian concept of marriage and the family in 2012 face challenges that Bavinck did not. However, in giving us a clear presentation of the Bible's teaching, of the reception thereof in the church's history, and further to that, a model of Christian theology applied to his own context, Bavinck has done us a great service.

In that regard, this book is an example to follow.

PREFACE
TO THE SECOND EDITION

Sooner than expected a second edition of this work about the Christian family has become necessary. The author felt no need to introduce important changes into this second edition. The alterations are therefore limited to a few linguistic improvements and to a clearer indication in the text of those places where we are moving to another topic within the chapters. In connection with the latter, the table of contents has been expanded.*

May this volume enjoy a favorable reception in many homes, and may it contribute to a greater appreciation of marriage and family life!

H. BAVINCK
Amsterdam, May 1912

---

* Ed. note: In the original Dutch, intentional blank line spaces within the chapters correlate to headings Bavinck added to the table of contents for the second edition. This older style has been updated in this English translation in that the headings from the table of contents now appear as regular headings within the chapters.

1

THE ORIGIN OF THE FAMILY

The Creation of Humanity, of Man and of Woman, in God's Image

The history of the human race begins with a wedding.

After God had created heaven and earth in the beginning, he conducted a six-day work project to prepare this creation to be humanity's home. For the heavens belong to the Lord, but the earth he has given to the children of men. That earth, however, had first existed in an unformed condition; it was untamed and empty. Through various separations or differentiations—between light and darkness, between the waters below and the waters above the firmament, between land and sea, between day and night, between months and years—God ended its wildness. And by populating land and sea, heaven and earth with a multitude of living creatures, plants and animals, fish and birds, God filled the creation and made its emptiness vanish.

This emptiness was fully overcome, however, only when God then proceeded to create humanity and the human race. For he did not create the earth so that it would remain empty, but he formed it so that people would inhabit the earth (Isa. 45:18). So he created this humanity after a special consultation; he created humanity according to his own image and likeness; he created humanity immediately as distinct sexes, as man and as woman. And when he had created them, he blessed them and gave them the whole earth as their territory.

Within these few features lies embedded everything we need to know about the origin, the essence, and the destiny of humanity. They contain a wisdom that far surpasses the understanding of the erudite. What Scripture furnishes us in the subsequent course of revelation, even already in the second chapter of the Bible, is mere expansion and explanation of what is told us crisply and briefly in the first chapter.

God first created man, his body coming from the dust of the earth, his soul created by the breath of life breathed in from above. The animals came into existence differently; at the powerful word of God they were brought forth through and from the earth. The angels also came into existence differently, for they were all created together, at once, perfect, in their full number. But man, related to both animals and angels, is nevertheless different from them. With the body, man stands in fellowship with the earth; with the spirit, which is from above, man is related to heaven. Both body and spirit are so intimately united within the human person that the human person possesses a unique nature and a unique position among all creatures. In a special sense a human person is a product of God; a person is his image and likeness, his child and his race.

The first human being, furthermore, was created immediately as a man, neither neuter nor androgynous, but with a specific sex. This came to expression in the fact that although he had been placed in the garden and had abundant provision of everything he needed for living, he nevertheless felt lonely. God created him this way; God says both to himself and from himself that it was not good that the man was alone. Immediately at creation God implanted within the man's soul the yearning for loving someone who would be like him. That yearning was not satisfied by the animals, whose essence he perceived, whose kinds he distinguished, and whose names he invented. They were strong and great, noble and magnificent, but they did not share his likeness. The creation of the woman was preceded by the sense of need, which the first man discovered in his own heart amid all his abundance; even having been created in God's image could not satisfy that need. So the woman is the answer to the question that flowed from the man's heart and across his lips. She is the answer to his prayer, the gift God so richly and lovingly bestowed upon him.

For although she was desired by the man, she was not created by him, but by God. The woman, just like the man, is a special creation of God, bearing his image and likeness. Even when the apostle Paul, in 1 Corinthians 11:7, calls the man the image and the glory of God, and the woman the glory of the man, he is certainly not thereby denying to the woman her creation in the image and likeness of God. For there he is not discussing the man and the woman as human beings in general, but rather the relationship of marriage within which they interact. Within married life and within the family, it is the husband as the head who in his appearance and glory radiates the image and glory of God; and the wife has the calling, in obedience to her husband, to display his glory. But this in no way contradicts the truth that the woman herself, seen as a human being, bears the image and likeness of God fully as much as the man does.

The creation story in Genesis shows this clearly in the fact that both together are said to have been created in God's image (Gen. 1:27). Not merely one of them, but both, and not the one separate from the other, but man and woman together, in mutual relation, each created in his or her own manner and each in a special dimension created in God's image and together displaying God's likeness. For this reason the Lord compares himself not only to a Father who takes pity on his children (Ps. 103:13), but also to a mother who cannot forget her nursing child (Isa. 49:15). He chastens like a father (Heb. 12:6), but he also comforts like a mother (Isa. 66:13), and replenishes for the loss of both (Ps. 27:10).

Each with His or Her Own Sex, Nature, and Position

Yet, even though the woman was not created *by* the man, she was nonetheless created *from* the man. Adam was made first, and then Eve. Both in time and in order, the man preceded the woman. The woman was created not merely *after* the man, but she was also brought forth *out of* the man. Just as the earth supplied the material for the man's body, so the man's body in turn supplied the material from which God formed the woman. The manner in which the man was created fixed an unbreakable bond between the human being and the earth; the manner in which the woman received her existence served to place her in the kind of relationship to the man such that she is inseparably bound to him, and thereby the unity of the human race is completely preserved. The woman was created not to be self-sufficient, nor to be independent of the man, nor apart from his mediation; she is not a unique principal and head of the human race, but she herself was formed out of the man, out of his flesh and blood. The human race is one entity, a body with one head, a building with one cornerstone.

In this reality the man finds no basis for pride, for he received the woman, whom he desired, entirely apart from his own effort, apart from his own knowledge and volition, while in a deep sleep, which God had placed upon his soul and body. Though the woman is indeed *from* the man, she did not come into being *through* him; her existence is due not to man, but just like man's existence, her existence is due entirely to God. In an absolute sense, then, she is a gift of God, the greatest gift that God could give to the man who had been created in his image—a gift that the man must therefore receive and value as given from the Lord's own hand.

This is also how Eve was greeted by Adam. As soon as he saw her, he recognized her; his recognition was a knowledge born of love. He saw in her no alien being, but a being just like himself; she possessed the same nature that he had; she displayed the same image of God that had been bestowed upon him; and yet she was different from him, with her own sex, character, and vocation. Like a whoop of joy, like a wedding song, the words came forth from his lips: This is now finally flesh of my flesh and bone of my bone; people will call her *manninne*,[1] because she came forth out of *man*!

Even as the man was created instantaneously, so too the woman was created instantaneously. Not only as a human being, but also as a woman, she found her origin in God. God is the Creator of the human being, and simultaneously also the Inaugurator of sex and of sexual difference. This difference did not result from sin; it existed from the very beginning, it has its basis in creation, it is a revelation of God's will and sovereignty, and is therefore wise and holy and good. Therefore, no one may misconstrue or despise this sexual difference, either within one's own identity or in that of another person. It has been willed by God and grounded in nature. It was then, and still is, willed by God; he is the sovereign Designer of sex; man and woman have God to thank not only for their human nature, but also for their different sexes and natures. Both are good, even as they both come forth from God's hand. Together in mutual fellowship they bear the divine image. God himself is the Creator of duality-in-unity.

Within that unity, they are and remain two. Each of the two has a unique nature, character, and vocation. Before the woman was created, the man had already been stationed in the garden and had been called to a particular task and vocation. As head of the human race, to him was given the probationary command, so that in keeping this command he would demonstrate his complete obedience to God. At the same time along with this command he received the task to cultivate and preserve the garden; the first included the

---

1 Ed. note: In Hebrew, *isha*, "woman," is the feminine form of *ish*, "man." The Statenvertaling (SV) uses *Manninne*, an otherwise nonexistent word, consisting of "man" with a feminine ending. The English word *woman* was in Old English *wifmon*, a combination of *wife* ("woman") and *man*. The rendering wo-man (with hyphen) seeks to show likewise that *Isha* is a derivative of *man*.

obligation to develop all the treasures that God had deposited in the earth; and the second involved the calling to protect the entire creation against every hostile power seeking to ruin the creation, and to preserve it from the tyranny of destructive forces. This twofold task—that of complete obedience to God, and that of cultivating and protecting the garden—was integrally related. A human being can be lord of the earth only when living as servant and child of God; only when the latter is true will a human being be able more and more to exercise dominion in the earth. The image of God unfolds in world lordship; the meek—those who perform God's will in obedience—inherit the earth.

If this is the calling of the image-bearer of God, however—namely, to fill the earth and to subdue it and exercise lordship in the earth—then the single individual person, even though he may be a man and a son of God, is not capable of exercising that calling. For that, he needs a helper; a woman, who does not stand above him to dominate him, nor beneath him as one degraded to the status of a tool for pleasure, but one who stands alongside him, stationed at his side and therefore formed from his side.

Man and woman are both human beings, and yet they are distinct in terms of physical build and psychological strength. So, even though they both receive the same calling, within that one calling each nevertheless receives a different task and activity. The man is called to subjugate under his feet the whole earth, in obedience to God's will; he must develop the earth in terms of its goals; through knowledge and art, through farming and animal husbandry, through industry and trade, he must bring forth from the earth all the riches of thought and power, of fruitfulness and life, which God has hidden within the earth according to his inscrutable goodness. And in voluntary obedience and dependent cooperation, the woman must assist in performing this task. Assist in the fullest and broadest sense, physically and spiritually, with her wisdom and love, with her head and her heart. Assist in procreating the human race, in nurturing children in the fear of the Lord, in fostering a kingdom of rational and moral citizens, and thereby assist in bringing the earth into subjection to the human race that comes forth from her.

Laboring Together in One Divine Task

For only in the human race is the image of God unfolded, and only in its dominion over the whole earth does the human race achieve its vocation and purpose. It is God himself who subdues the earth under his feet through the human race, and it is God himself who desires to display his own glory in the discovery of all of creation's treasures. Both—man and woman—stand thus with their distinct gifts in a united sacred service, both fulfill a shared precious calling, and labor at a single divine work. But they are able to respond to this their exalted vocation only when together they continue to obey the divine command, before everything else, to continue respecting the image of God in themselves and in each other, and as a consequence, keep living in the most intimate mutual fellowship. In order to make such unity, fellowship, and cooperation in soul and body both possible and real, God created the woman *from* the man and *for* the man (1 Cor. 11:8–9), but also simultaneously *unto* the man, even as he created the man *unto* the woman. God made two out of one, so that he could then make the two into one, one soul and one flesh. This kind of fellowship is possible only between two. From the very beginning, marriage was and is by virtue of its essential nature monogamous, an essential bond between one man and one woman, and therefore also a lifelong covenant, indissoluble by human authority; therefore what God has joined together, let not man put asunder (Matt. 19:6, 8). A man separates from his parents, forsakes father and mother, and cleaves to his wife; but he never abandons his wife! Love for parents is surpassed in both intensity and extent by love for one's wife. Such love is stronger than death. No other love resembles God's love so closely, or reaches such height.

Upon this fellowship of love, then, God has bestowed his blessing in a special way. He is the Creator of man and of woman, the

Inaugurator of marriage, and the Sanctifier of matrimony. Each child born is the fruit of fellowship, and as such is also the fruit of divine blessing. The two-in-oneness of husband and wife expands with a child into a three-in-oneness. Father, mother, and child are one soul and one flesh, expanding and unfolding the one image of God, united within threefold diversity and diverse within harmonic unity.

This three-in-oneness of relationships and functions, of qualities and gifts, constitutes the foundation of all of civilized society. The authority of the father, the love of the mother, and the obedience of the child form in their unity the threefold cord that binds together and sustains all relationships within human society. Within the psychological life of every integrated personality this triple cord forms the motif and melody. No man is complete without some feminine qualities, no woman is complete without some masculine qualities, and to both man and woman, the child is held up as an example (Matt. 18:3). These three characteristics and gifts are always needed in every society and in every civilization, in the church and in the state. Authority, love, and obedience are the pillars of all human society.

Somewhere a poet has celebrated the eternal-feminine. His poem could just as well have celebrated the eternal-masculine and the eternal-filial. For every good and perfect gift in man, woman, and child comes down from above, from the Father of lights, with whom there is no shadow or variation due to change (James 1:17). Every human being has been created—as a human being, but also as man or woman or child, each a self and yet in mutual fellowship—in the image of God.

2

THE DISRUPTION OF THE FAMILY

Sin and Its Consequences for Woman and for Man

The sin for which man, shortly after his creation, rendered himself culpable, affected the family in no small measure. The third chapter of Genesis tells us that the woman was tempted first. From this fact, together with the fact that Eve was created after Adam, Paul drew the conclusion that the woman may not serve as a teacher within the church and may not rule over the man (1 Tim. 2:12–14; cf. 1 Cor. 14:34). Naturally, the apostle does not mean to suggest thereby that Adam did not sin and was not culpable. For in Romans 5:12 he states that the one man, Adam, was responsible for all the sin and death in the world; in him and through him the entire human race fell; all people died in Adam on account of his sin (1 Cor. 15:22).

Paul did intend to say, however, that it was the woman who, at the very beginning, was the first to be tempted by the serpent, the first to fall personally, for herself; she was the first to become guilty of unbelief toward God and her husband, of gullibility toward the tempter. And her husband weakened in his faith and trust, because his wife tempted him and related to him as a teacher. Adam did not fall in the same way that Eve fell. Eve fell in terms of covetousness; she fell because she believed that eating the fruit would make her like God. Adam fell, however, because his love for his wife surpassed his love for God.

The first sin thus immediately involved a reversal within the family order. Rather than following her husband, the wife took the lead. Rather than being obedient, she took charge. Rather than being a helpmeet for him, she assumed the roles of mistress and regent. Adam and Eve sinned not only as individuals, as persons, but they sinned also as husband and wife, as father and mother; they were playing with their own destiny, with the destiny of their family, and with the destiny of the entire human race.

That became manifest immediately in the terrible consequences of their sin. The first manifestation of guilt came to expression in a sense of shame. Their eyes were opened at that point, and they became aware that they were naked. Shame is a sense of discomfort, a feeling of uneasiness, which consists particularly in fear of loss, something that overtakes us when we have done, or suppose we have done, something immodest. That immodesty can pertain to various things. A person is ashamed about something that should have remained behind the curtain of modesty and purity, something that has nevertheless been observed by others. A person is ashamed about something committed in violation of mores, customs, and forms of decency. A young person is frequently ashamed in front of friends on account of the good impulses arising from conscience. The "wise" and "understanding" are ashamed about the folly of the cross. The pious are ashamed before God and others on account of the sins they have committed.

In the third chapter of Genesis, however, we are told that Adam and Eve were ashamed because they were naked. Nakedness could not have been the deepest source of their shame, however, for they had been naked before their sin and had not been ashamed of it. Their sense of guilt did indeed come to focus on their nakedness, in that they acquired a sense of uneasiness, an uncomfortable feeling, but this did not originate in nakedness itself. It had a deeper source. They had transgressed God's command, and were no longer innocent—neither toward God nor toward each other. Their eyes were opened; they no longer dared to look each other in the eye; they read one another's guilt on the other's face and they heard its echo all around them in all of nature. A terrible change had occurred in the condition of their souls, and so they viewed everything differently—themselves, each other, the world around them, and especially God. They did not dare to see him, they fled from his face, and hid among the trees of the garden. Their eyes had indeed been opened, but in a different sense than the tempter had promised.

Yet, that shame is also a blessing. An animal knows no shame, and the devil even less. Shame is unique to humanity, to fallen humanity disobedient to God's command, something that humanity also senses and recognizes. Shame is a sign of an awakened conscience, that human capacity which pronounces a person guilty and condemns him. Through the function of conscience a person retains something that disapproves of sin, something that stands as a judge over and against a person, something that removes the peace, rest, and contentment on account of the transgression that has been committed. That person is doubly wounded who silences his conscience, who hardens and sears his conscience, which leads ultimately to living without a conscience and without shame! Even though our conscience pains us and condemns us, conscience binds us to the world of unseen things and restrains us from sinking into bestiality. And what the conscience does for us inwardly in the soul, shame performs for us outwardly in the body. Shame has been described, not without cause, as the body's conscience. Both conscience and shame demonstrate the brokenness and disintegration of human existence, the disharmony of human life, the distance between what a person ought to be and what a person really is. Both point back to that disruptive event at the beginning of history, when humanity fell from the height occupied at creation, and descended from the vocation to which humanity had been called.

Conscience and shame together drive a person to cover himself and to conceal himself. Nakedness began to be a hindrance, because people had lost their innocence. Losing the garment of righteousness made clothes necessary as covering. For human beings, conscience, shame, and clothing are intimately related. Together they serve to remind us of our God-created beginning and of our deepest fall; they presuppose our guilt and preserve our humanness; they simultaneously oppress us and liberate us. All three distinguish human beings from angels and animals, and provide human beings a unique position in creation. They proclaim humanity's need for—and capacity for—salvation. They create for humanity a domain between hell and heaven; they preserve human beings outside Paradise for atonement through the cross.

The Punishment of Sin for Each, and the Related Blessing

The punishment pronounced upon humanity after their transgression points in this same direction. This is true not only of the punishment given to the serpent, which established a division between the seed of the serpent and the seed of the woman, which broke apart the covenant between mankind and Satan and brought about in its place God's covenant with humanity. This is true as well of the particular punishments placed upon the woman and the man, punishments related to the nature and calling of each, punishments that had very serious consequences for the history of the family.

Eve was punished not only as a human being, but particularly as mother and as wife—something that reveals a divine ordinance. God punished the first human beings in terms of their respective sins. The woman had abused her calling to be a helper suited to her husband, by tempting him and leading him to fall. So she is punished in terms of this her calling. She is punished as *mother*, since that which was to have been a wife's greatest delight would become her greatest pain. From this time forward, she cannot fulfill her calling apart from leading a life of continual physical and spiritual pain. And yet she can neither desert this calling nor liberate herself from it, for she remains *woman*; despite the pain-filled life that will be her portion in marriage, all the desires of her soul move her to fulfill her calling; she remains bound to her husband, and longs to be joined with him.

The man was punished already in this punishment of the woman. For even as she with respect to him, so he with respect to her has lost his freedom, his independence, his self-direction. Slave of his longings, he becomes slave to the woman, in order thereafter to avenge his humiliation and self-debasement in angry tyranny. Driven to the man through her own desire, the woman seeks with her wiles to enchant him, or she bows like a slave under his feet. Slavery and tyranny are the sins to which the mutual relationship of man and woman have been consigned and exposed since the violation of God's ordinances.

In addition to this, however, the man receives his own punishment, which affects him in his particular calling, namely, working in the sweat of his brow. On account of man, the ground is cursed, so that by itself it brings forth only thorns and thistles; the creation is subjected to vanity, not for its own sake but for the sake of him who subjected it; and all of nature is changed into a power that opposes humanity with a hostility that oppresses human existence and human living. When humanity breaks its bond with God, its harmony with the world is broken. Thus the man must go forth to subdue the earth along the path of continual wrestling; he must engage in contending against the frightening powers of nature, the raging elements, the mauling animals, the inhospitable terrain, against wind and weather, cold and heat, rock and dirt. He must work with head and hand, full of pain and trouble, each day, his entire life. He must conquer the world and render nature serviceable one foot at a time, one step at a time. Only in this way, by the sweat of his brow, can the man keep himself alive, along with his family and the entire human race. From now on, hunger and love drive him restlessly onward.

This punishment is also a blessing, however, for the individual man, for the family, and for all of society. For it includes, first, that the man will continue living, that he will not immediately fall prey to death, as he had deserved, that he would be fruitful, would multiply, and would fill the earth with his race. With that expectation, the first man changed the name of his wife. She had earlier been called *Manninne*, because she was taken from the man and was given to him as a helpmeet. Now she will bear the name of *Eve*, mother of the living, because the woman gives way to the mother, and her assistance to the man is now rendered as the one who bears and nurtures children.

Furthermore, humanity retains the task entrusted to it at the beginning of creation. Humanity continues to be called to fill the earth, to subdue it, and to exercise dominion. Even though humanity can answer this calling in no other way than partially and through fearsome struggle, this trouble-filled labor is in itself a blessing, because it maintains humanity in its exaltedness above nature, and preserves humanity in the face of spiritual and moral defeat. Finally, there lies embedded within these punishments also the promise that God will accompany humanity along its difficult journey and will strengthen and support humanity in fulfilling its calling. For Eve is the mother of life, she carries life in her womb, the life of humanity, the life of the seed of the woman. The woman will be saved through bearing children; in her womanly and motherly calling she will display her most beautiful and most elegant virtues, not only, but Mary, the one blessed among women, will also repair Eve's offense. In the Son born from her, the woman and the man once again attain to their calling; for in Christ, the servant of the Lord, not only does the labor of his soul restore the truth and achieve reconciliation, but also overcomes the world.

To Adam and Eve with their offspring, the holy family of Joseph, Mary, and the child form the divine counterpart.

3

THE FAMILY AMONG THE NATIONS

The Ravaging of the Family through Sin

The descent of the human race from one set of parents included the fact that the sons and daughters of Adam and Eve, who were thus brothers and sisters, entered into marriage with each other. At that point this marriage of brothers and sisters was not incest, since their mutual relationship could not yet have been set off and demarcated from that with other families. Only later when many families had come into existence could the notion have arisen that brothers and sisters relate differently toward each other than toward the children born of different parents and descended from different families. At that time, under God's direction and through the beneficial care of his providence, that deep and ineradicable feeling of blood relationship and awareness of incestuous relationships was planted within the human heart, which functions as one of the most powerful bulwarks for the protection of the family and for the bridling of unrighteousness. For from the beginning it was the will of God that, as soon as more families arose, the man would *leave* his father and mother and would choose a wife as his helpmeet not from within but from outside the parental family, from another family. The wonderful expansion of the human race, the infinite variety among people, and the inexhaustible richness of relationships between households and families, generations and peoples, are all due to this divine will. Every marriage blends various psychological gifts and distinct physical strengths, becoming thereby a new source of a particular fullness of life.

But sin immediately exercised its destructive effect on the home. It had already introduced disunity between Adam and Eve, and caused the husband to blame his wife [Gen. 3:12]. It filled Cain with hatred against Abel and incited him to fratricide [Gen. 4:8]. It led Lamech into polygamy, and enticed him, in his song in praise of the sword, to boast in that glorious invention of Tubal-cain [Gen. 4:23–24]. Thanks to that invention, he now possessed weapons with which he was able to avenge himself up to seventy-seven times against everyone who assaulted him or one of his people! Revenge and the thirst for revenge were the inspiration behind the first song that we hear from the lips of fallen man. And the subsequent chapters of Genesis leading up to the flood narrate for us the growth and spread of sin to which humanity surrendered during that period. Godlessness and immorality went hand in hand. They ate, drank, married, and were given in marriage until the day when Noah entered the ark and the flood came and destroyed all of them.

After the flood the descendants of Noah, who at that point still constituted one people and were still bound together by one language and by the same vocabulary, settled in the land of Shinar, which lay in southern Babylonia. But then later, as punishment for building the tower, their language was confused, and the small human race was split up into groups, tribes, or nations and dispersed from Babylonia across the entire earth. From then on, every nation went its own way and underwent its own development. All of them took along from their common dwelling place a treasury of traditions and ideas, morals and customs, abilities and capacities, which have been partially preserved in the culture of the nations. But they nevertheless moved away from each other, and gradually became more isolated from each other, eventually becoming frequent enemies of one another. A significant portion of human history involves warfare among tribes, races, and nations. Therefore the life of marriage and family naturally developed among the various peoples in quite different ways. One cannot put all the peoples from different regions of the earth and in various periods of history on one line and treat them all in the same way. There were peoples whose family life displayed a relative purity and chastity, and there were others among whom it was perverted in a terrible manner. Even among the same people favorable and unfavorable circumstances appeared together, just as now and then by virtue of special circumstances a people can experience moral improvement, so too it happens not infrequently that a people that has achieved a high level of flourishing and welfare nonetheless through prosperity and abundance has deteriorated and declined in terms of religion and morality, in terms of home life and family life. The eye of the historian must always be unprejudiced and fully open for assessing this extraordinarily great diversity of life.

The Origin and Development of the Family according to the Teaching of Evolution

Today, however, people violate this simple and yet so irrefutable law in the most egregious manner. Under the influence of the teaching of evolution, people have charted a course in terms of the idea that the entire human race and each nation in particular has undergone its own process of development, and done so by necessity. The stations along that route are identified with great precision and are named as follows. First there existed among people in the realm of sexual life nothing other than *promiscuity* and *concubinage*. People descended, according to the claim of the evolutionists, from the animals. It cannot be claimed with certainty whether they came from one or from multiple pairs, in one or in multiple regions of the earth. But in any case, they descended from animals, and very gradually became separated from their origin and elevated above their ancestors, and for centuries remained half-animal. In this way they lived together like the animals of the field; there was no marriage and no home whatsoever; and there was no such thing as incest, prostitution, and adultery. Every man belonged to every woman, and every woman belonged to every man. People identify this situation of completely unordered sexual living governed entirely by lust with the term *promiscuity*, completely free sexual relationships.

Nevertheless, from the very beginning already those animal-humans needed each other, not only for satisfying their sexual impulse, but also to supply provisions for living and to protect their own existence against the destructive power of nature or the attacks of wild animals. In this way a certain form of communal living gradually developed. Home and family did not yet exist; parental and filial love were still entirely unknown; a sense of shame was still virtually alien to those first people. But like many animal species, they lived together in groups; the *horde* was the original, earliest form of communal living, from which a complex, richly layered society gradually emerged during a period of hundreds and thousands of centuries. The children who were born belonged not to the father or mother, but to the horde, and were included in the tribal community from birth.

Sexual relations occurred initially between men and women who belonged to the same horde or troupe. But that gradually changed. It could happen, for example, that within the circle of one's own horde there were not enough women or that men desired women who belonged to another horde. Then men would go alone or in league with others or perhaps as an entire horde of men to steal the women of another troupe. Such kidnapping of women often occurred on a wide scale, with severe and bloody fighting. The memory of that ancient situation is still preserved among many peoples in terms of women being purchased for a considerable sum, or being purchased by means of a simulated sale and a dowry. But this kidnapping of women and the subsequent sexual relations with women from another horde or tribe had the additional consequence that within the circle of the horde community another sentiment began to form, namely, the sense of *kinship* and *blood relationship.* This sense was extremely important, since it became the source of a unique and new development. When this sense arose, the human race entered upon a new path, the path of living as families in distinction from living as hordes.

This blood kinship, however, was initially identified only through the mother. For marriage did not yet exist; the man satisfied his lust but did not live alongside and with the woman with whom he had bonded for that one moment. But the woman became a mother; she kept the child with her, at least for a time after the child's birth. That child needed his or her mother for food and assistance, and otherwise would have perished. In this way the bond between mother and child was much more close, intimate, and strong than that between the father and the child; in fact, that latter relationship did not even exist in the beginning. The father was and remained unknown, but everyone knew who the child's mother was. In this way the child was identified through the mother; the mother was the boss within the home; she was the one who first gave shape to family life and home life, and initially had authority in everything. In this period of development, consequently, there existed a *matriarchy* and even a *feminocracy.* That period was the ideal time for women, for they possessed a power that later they would never again share.

But this period of feminine domination came to an end. There was a kind of family life with the woman at the head. But the man was still absent; he was not yet part of the family. On the contrary, at that point the woman did not yet have one husband, but she had many men, first one then another (called *polyandry*), who visited her and abandoned her, spending their time not in the family, but in wide open nature or in each other's company, occupying themselves especially with hunting and fishing. But this nomadic life gradually transitioned to a settled life; hunting and fishing gave way to agriculture and animal husbandry. Thereby men became connected more closely to the home, and they gradually continued living with the women they had taken, and with the children they had fathered. When in this way they became more connected to their home, and through their labor provided support to the family, at that point the power of the woman gradually shifted to the man. The men began gradually and inevitably, or by force and design, to push the women into the background, to oppress them and to make them their slaves. The domination of women was replaced by the domination of men; slowly matriarchy gave way to *patriarchy*.

This patriarchal period was characterized by the father possessing all authority and power in the family. The wife, children, slaves, house, animals, fields, etc., were all *his* property; he could do with them as he pleased, and even had authority over the freedom and the life of his wives and children. Not only could he take as many wives as he wished (*polygamy*, instead of the earlier polyandry), but he could also send them away, sell them, divorce them, whatever pleased him. But this situation was not destined to survive. For living in such a sumptuous manner was possible only for a few, but the simple citizens and the poor could not support so many wives and children; they were naturally compelled by circumstances to live with one woman. In the practical matters of life itself polygamy gave way to *monogamy*, the marriage of one man to one woman. This practice was subsequently established theoretically and elevated in many civilized countries to the level of law.

The Inaccuracy of This Construction

This in brief is the understanding of the developmental process of marriage and family formed by people in the circles of evolutionists. People cannot refrain from boasting about how marriage and family were ingeniously invented and expertly constructed. One thing is lacking, however—namely, the foundation on which they rest, the reality by which they must be supported. This has slowly come to be acknowledged once again by experts. For a long time people surrendered to this understanding driven by the illusion that in this way they could explain fully the rich history of family living. But further and deeper investigation has exposed its untenability. Not long ago a Dutch scientist claimed that nowadays people usually no longer believe that promiscuity was the origin of human sexual life, that communal property preceded private property, that feminocracy formed the beginning of all civilization, that fear of death and respect for ancestors was the origin of all religion. In general people have become more cautious in applying the theory of evolution. Their eyes have been opened more and more to the diversity of life. To identify peoples and situations simply in a predetermined order *after* one another, like exhibits in a museum, does violence to the reality and the pluriformity of life.

In one respect the above-mentioned theory has yielded benefit and registered some gain. Better than we formerly knew or could have known, it has shed light through the study of anthropology and cultural history on the tragic manner in which marriage and family life have been disrupted by sin. We hardly encounter this disruption strictly in this area alone, but everywhere throughout human life. We are guilty of extreme imbalance if we view sins against the seventh commandment as the worst and most serious, and consider those against the other commandments to be less serious. This imbalance comes out even in our use of the word *immorality*, for all of the Ten Commandments belong to the moral law and regulate our morals, yet we think this word refers almost exclusively to transgressions of the seventh commandment. Nevertheless, we may never forget that the sins of idolatry, image worship, defiling God's name and God's day, undermining authority, etc., in principle demonstrate a more serious character than sexual immorality and adultery. Spiritual sins like unbelief, denying God, pride, avarice, greed, ambition, hatred of God and neighbor, etc., are no less deserving of punishment in the eyes of the Lord than the sins of the flesh. It is indeed proof of the darkening of our understanding and the wicked thoughts of our heart when we view the latter as far worse than the former, and allow ourselves to be guided in our judgment about people and situations by this unspiritual perspective.

Nevertheless, for us sensual people, the destruction arising from sin is manifest especially in sexual practices. Here it appears most clearly on the outside, in full light; here it can as it were be touched with our hands. There is no need to investigate that disruption in extensive detail, mentioning all the coarse and refined sins committed against the seventh commandment. All the rich, glorious relationships that God originally created as part of the life of marriage, home, and family—between husband and wife, parents and children, brothers and sisters, those free and those who are servants—are attacked and disrupted by those sins. An entire army of evils besieges the life of the family: the infidelity of the husband, the stubbornness of the wife, the disobedience of the child; both the worship and the denigration of the woman, tyranny as well as slavery, the seduction and the hatred of men, both idolizing and killing children; sexual immorality, human trafficking, concubinage, bigamy, polygamy, polyandry, adultery, divorce, incest; unnatural sins whereby men commit scandalous acts with men, women with women, men with boys, women with girls, men and women and children with each other, people with animals; the stimulation of lust by impure thoughts, words, images, plays, literature, art, and clothing; glorifying nudity and elevating even the passions of the flesh into the service of deity—all of these and similar sins threaten the existence and undermine the well-being of the home.

When the evolutionists bring up these facts from the history of the human race, they simply expose this tragic reality. But they err when they claim that these are the result and outworking of an animal-like situation in which people lived originally. For even if we wanted to leave out of consideration for a moment the testimony of Scripture that speaks of an entirely different beginning of humanity, even then this understanding is powerfully and loudly contradicted by history. For these terrible sins hardly appear only and in the most extreme measure among the coarsest of people, but they are found in their most rampant forms among civilized and developed societies. And if one wishes to uncover and observe them here, then one must go not to the isolated, tranquil villages, but to the center of civilization, to the focal points of culture, to the large cities full of grandeur and glory. There one finds them, indeed, among the coarse masses, but just as prevalent and in refined form among the upper echelons of society, in the palaces, in the salons, in the corridors of art. Occasionally, once in a while, such sins emerge into view in connection with a lawsuit, a scandal, a locale. It becomes manifest what a world of unrighteousness lies hidden beneath the varnished exterior of a civilization. When the evolutionists understand all these terrible situations to be atavism, to be the outworking of an animal-like past, then they undermine the concept of sin, turn wickedness into a sickness, change the sense of guilt into an illusion, turn prisons into hospitals, and they thereby do an injustice to the animal world. For animals do not live as people often live with and among each other. In order to sin in such a terrible and refined manner, one must be a human being. Even the nature of sin and the manner of sinning demonstrate that one is a human being and was originally created not in the image of the ape, but in the image of God.

The Preserving of Marriage and Family Life among All Peoples, Despite Its Frequent and Serious Perversion

But now we see the miraculous arise in this sad history. Despite all those grievous sins that besieged and disrupted the home for century after century, generation after generation, among all peoples and in every land, despite this entire stream of evils, the home has been preserved and maintained everywhere and in every age in more or less pure form. The advocates of the teaching of evolution claim otherwise, and they argue that there was no evidence of home and family life at the beginning of the human race and even today among many tribes and peoples. But this is pure fantasy; a careful study of reality teaches something entirely different, and acquaints us with the surprising fact that the fundamental ordinances of family life still appear even among the peoples who are the most undeveloped. With a view to the above-mentioned sins it would hardly be surprising if it were different, and if here and there an isolated tribe or people had lost every notion of marital and family life. But that is *not* the case; that this is not the case is a miracle, and becomes more miraculous to the extent that we reflect more deeply about it. It is a miracle of God's grace and of the leading of his providence.

For we encounter everywhere, to a weaker or stronger degree, home and family life. We encounter among all peoples laws, mores, customs, and usages either described or undescribed, that regulate entrance into marriage, the relationship between husband and wife, and the relationship between parents and children. The sense of shame belongs to all people by nature; it is not absent even among those peoples whose clothing consists exclusively in the covering of nakedness; and the notion of incest is stronger among numerous simple people groups than among civilized nations. In addition, various disordered situations of unchastity and immorality do indeed appear, but these are found just as frequently among civilized people and have absolutely no persuasive force contradicting the existence of such laws and regulations. If some have thought that completely free sexual relations was the practice among a few tribes and was the original lifestyle of the human race, then that view rests on defective observation and a premature conclusion. Since pairing and a kind of society appears among the more developed animals, Darwin himself disagrees that promiscuity was the earliest situation of the human race. Many who otherwise are devoted to the teaching of evolution join him in judging that the society of the earliest humans can have begun very well with marriage and family. It appears to have been and still to be the custom among several tribes that at most the young men and women may engage in sexual relations with each other freely before marriage. But this form of promiscuity is far from established, and in any case appears only here and there, and gives way to marriage as the basis of an ordered society. The theory that the human race began with promiscuity and subsequently traversed a period of polyandry and polygamy, in order along this route to arrive at monogamy, has been almost universally surrendered. Neither the human race in its entirety nor each people group in particular has passed all these stations along the way; in the experience of the human race, the situations identified by this theory do not arise *after* each other, but always arise *alongside* each other.

Furthermore, the distinction between man and woman was always known among all people groups, and taken into account by all of them in terms of practice. Nature teaches this distinction, and no science or philosophy is needed to acquaint oneself with this. Man and woman differ in physical structure and physical strength, in psychological nature and psychological strength; thereby they naturally enjoy different rights and are called to different duties; no single people was unfamiliar with this and did not organize the practical matters of life accordingly. From the very beginning there existed a kind of division of labor both before marriage and within marriage. In the main, that division of labor came down to this, that the man took care of obtaining food from the animal world while the woman took care of obtaining food from the plant world. The man tilled the land, the woman tended the livestock. The man performed his work by going away from home, occasionally far away, and the woman performed her work in the home or in the neighborhood of her dwelling.

Various circumstances could occasion change in these practices. For example, if people lived in a fertile region and a warm climate, such that little work was needed to provide for the necessities of life, then the man often surrendered to laziness and left all the work to the woman. Or also, if work was viewed as something despicable, as was the case among many people groups, and only hunting and capturing were deemed worthy for a man, then the woman came to occupy a position of oppression and was denigrated to a means of pleasure, to a slave, and to merchandise. But thereby it could also happen that the woman at home achieved a great degree of independence and freedom, acquiring a capacity and achieving rights that strengthened her position with respect to the man who was living away from home and was hardly involved with his family.

In the formal sense, however, a feminocracy never existed anywhere. Naturally the woman never lacked power and influence over her children, her husband, and her entire family. Here and there she was even called to fill important and dignified posts, so that from time to time queens have governed among various nations. But this is exceptional and something entirely different than a formal feminocracy. Always and everywhere the man has been the head of the family. Among some nations or at least among some classes it was customary to identify the name, the status, and the family of the child in terms of the mother. Blood relationship was viewed more intimately and more highly than marital community; having been born of the same mother constituted true relatedness. In fact, we read in Genesis that the man must *leave* his father and mother and as it were, follow his wife; among Israel heavy emphasis was placed upon blood relationship through one's mother, and even to this day the proverb is well known among us that one loses a son to marriage, but with a daughter's marriage one gains a son. But all of this has nothing to do with feminocracy. Even where relationship is identified according to blood, that is, according to the mother, the man was nevertheless head of the family, protector of his wife, father of his children, owner of his land, representative in the council, participant in war. The number of writers is not small who, over against defenders of matriarchy and feminocracy, insist that patriarchy was the earliest form of family life.

Concubinage and polygamy are closely connected with this patriarchy. Indeed, these are encountered among many people groups in antiquity and in the present time. It was an evil hour when Muhammad permitted it out of self-interest, in the context of his sensual religion, and thereby unleashed a torrent of family distress among his followers. Missionaries must continually contend with this deeply rooted evil. But still one must beware of exaggeration at this point. In antiquity monogamy was the rule among the Babylonians, the Egyptians, the Greeks, and the Romans; even where law or custom permitted the man to take concubines, one woman continued as his actual spouse. Both polygamy and monogamy appear among primitive people groups; the Indians in California, the Veddas of Ceylon, the inhabitants of the Andaman and Nicobar Islands, and many others both knew and respected the marriage of one man and one woman. Even where polygamy was lawful, ordinarily one woman continued to be adorned with privilege, and concubinage was customary only among the prominent men, the wealthy folk, because lesser citizens could not afford such luxury. Frequently we encounter the phenomenon that among various people groups, a higher respect for marriage and family life is seen the more deeply we investigate their past, whereas with the increase of well-being and wealth such respect deteriorates and is assaulted and oppressed by means of various ignoble practices.

When we take all of this into consideration, we are not puzzled by the fact that family life among the nations has supplied us with a rich and glorious poetry. In Egypt, in Greece, and especially in Rome, the woman was held in high honor, at least in antiquity. The Chinese can be examples for us of respect for parents. Numerous histories from the life of the nations speak to us of intimate love between husband and wife, between parents and children. Literature and art bring to our view various scenes of masculine fidelity, feminine devotion, and filial dependence. The legislation, for example, of Hammurabi, known for several years now, is comparable at several points to that of Moses; it contains various stipulations that protected the married woman in relation to her husband, especially in case of divorce. After the fall, God did not abandon humanity; within the heart of husband and wife, of parents and children, he preserved the natural love that he had planted in that heart, and thereby opened a fountain of pure happiness and inestimable blessing for earthly life.

4

THE FAMILY IN ISRAEL

Law and Custom among Israel with Regard to Marriage, Patriarchy, Paternal Authority, Women, and Children

The distinction between Israel and the other nations is more clearly evident from the first table of the Law than from the second table. The revelation to the patriarchs and to the nation descended from them consisted first of all in the truth that God the Almighty, who certified his eternal faithfulness in the name Jehovah, made himself known to them and entered with them into an unbreakable covenant. But if God bestowed himself in grace to Israel in this way, then Israel ought to serve God alone, who led them out of Egypt, and have no other gods before him. Although all the nations around Israel became ensnared more and more tightly in superstition, this people received from the Lord's hand at the same time a law that proscribed all idolatry and image worship, all sorcery and magic, all veneration of stars and spirits. When Israel entered Canaan, she was tempted every moment by the nations living around her to serve Jehovah by means of an image or to serve other gods altogether. But there always remained a smaller or larger group devoted to the service of the Lord and to his law. From that sacred, pious circle came the sages and the prophets, the poets of the psalms and proverbs.

But the first table of the Law is followed by the second; the great commandment comes first, but is followed by another; love toward God is the foundation and the principle undergirding love toward the neighbor. This neighbor love is not prescribed for the first time in the New Testament (Matt. 22:39), but was known as God's command in the period of the old covenant as well [Lev. 19:18]. Such love was not to consist exclusively in an external rendering of service, but was supposed to be a matter of the heart (Lev. 19:11–17), and even supposed to suppress and eradicate all covetous desire for the neighbor's property. In all of her walk and talk, Israel was supposed to be a holy people, a kingdom of priests, such that all might freely approach God and be separate from all the nations (Exod. 19:6). This principle undergirded the legislation for marriage and family as well, even though in terms of the dispensations of history, it reached complete fulfillment for the first time in the New Testament.

Patriarchy existed among Israel from the earliest time, such that we usually speak of the period of the patriarchs. This patriarchal arrangement, however, was hardly restricted to the pre-Mosaic period, but was both assumed by and assimilated into the law, and was perpetuated throughout Israel's subsequent history. The entire organization of the nation was along patriarchal lines, arranged in terms of the principle of genealogical descent. The twelve tribes, among whom Judah was preeminent, were divided into clans, the clans into extended families, and these extended families into households. Each of those groups had its own head, representative, or prince; and all these heads or princes together formed the "members of the assembly." When they gathered, the "congregation" of Israel was gathered. So properly speaking, a national government power did not exist among Israel; later, when the people wanted and received a king, this did not destroy the patriarchal order but allowed it to continue, so that it now needed to be factored in (1 Kings 12). The nation remained in all respects bound to the law of God, for God was the proper Lawgiver, Judge, and King of Israel (Deut. 17:19-20; Isa. 33:22).

For this reason, the authority and power of the home rested with the father. Great significance was attached to the blood relationship via the mother. The expression "sons of my mother" occurs several times (Gen. 43:29). Abraham was married to his half sister, the daughter of his father, so that kinship from the side of the father by itself was no impediment to marriage (Gen. 20:12). Laban tells Jacob, the son of his sister: You are my bone and my flesh (Gen. 29:14). Abimelech talks in the same way to the citizens of the city of his mother's birth (Judg. 9:1-2). And according to the levirate law, the brother of a man who died childless, who was born of the same mother, was supposed to marry the widow of his deceased brother and produce offspring for his brother. But all of this did not at all lead to the disappearance of patriarchy; the father was the king, the master within his family (Gen. 18:12).

As such, the husband and father possessed extensive power. In addition to his lawful wife he could take one or more concubines; the law permitted this patriarchal custom to exist and did not forbid polygamy (Lev. 18:18; Deut. 21:15). He had the right to divorce his wife if he had found "something shameful" with her (Deut. 24:1). The power to give his children in marriage rested with him (Gen. 24:3; Judg. 14:1-5), to invalidate the vow of his wife or daughter under certain conditions (Num. 30), to bring a dissolute and rebellious son to the elders of the city (Deut. 21:18-19). In general the duty of guarding the honor of his family, administering its property, advancing its welfare, and leading it in the fear of the Lord rested with the husband. Family and wife, male and female slaves, ox and donkey were all *his* property (Exod. 20:17). The home, the entire family constituted one organic unit, with the patriarch as head. Along with this head, all the members, and along with the father, the entire family, were either blessed or punished (Exod. 20:5–6).

Nevertheless one would be mistaken to conclude from this extensive power of the head of the family that his wife and children lived in a situation of slavery. Of course, men among Israel, just like men among other nations, occasionally abused their power; but such abuse occurred always and everywhere, including in our society, without the law being able to do much to change that; sin always finds an escape route. But the expression that in the patriarchal family, the man was the master of the family, that wife and children were his property like the house and the slave, hardly proves that the man stood in the same relation toward all these "possessions," and was allowed to exercise the same power and arbitrariness toward all of them. The absence of laws describing the rights of wives and children provides no basis for arguing that in reality they were devoid of all rights, and were handed over to their master's kindness or lack thereof.

Nowadays people frequently allege that conclusion, but this view proceeds from the theory of evolution, which teaches that on its own, nature is chaotic, a disorderly situation, a battle of everyone against everyone else, and that in such a situation order is created only through the legislation of the state. The man is viewed essentially as a wild animal that is tamed and turned into a man only by the state. The state becomes the great domesticator and nurturer of humanity, the source of all rights, the creator and shaper of society. But this perspective is pervasively false, for it fails to take into account the rational and moral nature of human beings, their reason and conscience, their heart and soul—in short, the creation and providence of God. Rather than concluding from the limited number or complete absence of laws that people live in a situation without rights, in many cases we can with more warrant argue just the reverse and say: the more laws we need, the more it becomes evident that rational and moral understanding, that natural love and natural bonds, are losing their influence and power. If in the present day the rights of the wife, of the child, of the servant, and of the laborer

The Family in Israel

must be established by law, then surely this can be explained as due largely to self-interest undermining the moral character of society. Among Israel, the rights of the wife and the children, and actually those of the husband as well, were established in large part not in the law but in the mores. Those mores ascribed to the wife and children a large measure of independence. Daughters enjoyed significant freedom in the home, and dealt in an unsophisticated manner with strangers (Gen. 24:15-16; 29:10; Exod. 2:16; Judg. 14:1; 1 Sam. 9:11; etc.). The husband was the head of the family and master of the wife; but when in Exodus 20:17 the law speaks of the neighbor's wife, then from that it hardly follows at all that the wife is his property in the same sense as his ox or his donkey, even as when today a husband speaks about *his* wife or a wife about *her* husband or a doctor about *his* patients and a lawyer about *his* clients. Wives like Sarah, Rebekah, Rachel, Hannah, Abigail, etc., hardly give the impression of having been slaves; they are free women who are honored and loved by their husbands. Although they spent most of their time in the home, they went about without veils and freely in their dealings with men (Gen. 12:14; Ruth 2:5-6; 2 Sam 20:16), took part in feasts (Exod. 15:20-21; Judg. 16:27; 1 Sam. 18:6-7), occasionally brought their own possessions into marriage, such as slaves, which subsequently remained in their possession (Gen. 16:2, 6; 24:8; 29:24, 29; 30:4, 9).

In the home the wife had her own task; she was charged with care for the housekeeping, and thus kept busy with spinning and weaving, sewing and making clothes, baking bread and caring for the flock (Gen. 29:9; Exod. 2:16; 1 Sam. 2:19; 8:13; 2 Sam. 13:8; Prov. 31:10-31). Alongside her husband she assumed care of the feeding and nurture of the children. Since the wife achieved her full honor only as mother, she fervently desired children, especially sons (Gen. 16; 1 Sam. 1), and viewed having them as a rich treasure, as a blessing and inheritance of the Lord (Ps. 127:3). The firstborn son was the embodiment of masculine strength, the heir of paternal authority, the advocate on behalf of his mother and sister (Gen. 27:29, 37; 49:3, 8; Deut. 21:15-17).

The Nurture of Children, the Position of the Woman, and the Sanctity of Marriage

All of those children must be nurtured in the fear and knowledge of the ways of the Lord (Exod. 20:2; 12:26; Deut. 4:9; etc.), and were obligated to show honor and respect to their parents and to all the elderly. The mother was not forgotten in this regard (Exod. 20:12), but in Leviticus 19:3[1] was seen as even more important than the father; striking or cursing father or mother was punished with death (Exod. 21:15; Lev. 20:9). In Proverbs 31:10–31, Lemuel sings in praise of the competent and industrious homemaker. Her value is greater than that of rubies. Her children rise up and call her blessed, as does her husband, who praises her, saying: "Many women have done excellently, but you surpass them all. Charm is deceitful, and beauty is vain, but a woman who fears the LORD is to be praised" [vv. 29–30]. Among Israel the wives participated in the days of rest and the feast days, in the sacrifices and temple singing. They were not entirely and completely excluded even from public life; Miriam and Deborah, Huldah and Noadiah functioned among the people as prophetesses, and queens Jezebel and Athaliah led the people in the service of idols.

Moreover, among Israel marriage was a civic institution, so much so that the law made no mention of any religious act to be performed when entering marriage, although this would not have been omitted in practice. But nevertheless marriage was of divine origin, instituted by God (Gen. 1:27), in principle and in essence monogamous and unbreakable (Gen. 2:18–24), a covenant established by God (Prov. 2:17; Hosea 2:18; Ezek. 16:8; Mal. 2:14). For that reason it was supposed to be kept sacred. The law did indeed permit polygamy and divorce; but these occurred because of the hardness of heart, conflicted with the essence of marriage, and

---

[1] Ed. note: Original reads "Leviticus 9:3" but is a typo. Bavinck is noting the importance placed on the mother in this verse, which reverses the usual "father or mother" order of these laws: "Every one of you shall revere his mother and his father."

were never the rule. Following the example of the patriarchs, kings and nobles later used that freedom, but ordinary citizens had only one wife. Prophets and poets proceeded from the idea that marriage was a bond between one man and one woman (Hosea 1–3; Prov. 12:4; 18:22; 19:14; 31:10–31), and in the Greek translation of the Old Testament the words from Genesis 2:24, *they* shall be one flesh, are translated as *those two* shall be one flesh—a translation adopted in the New Testament (Matt. 19:5; Mark 10:8; 1 Cor. 6:16; Eph. 5:31).

Furthermore, respect for the home was established by a number of stipulations that proscribed marital relationships between blood relatives and members of the immediate family, and those were esteemed so highly that they are followed and adopted not only in ecclesiastical but also in civil legislation. Forbidden with equal vigor were prostitution (Gen. 38:24; Lev. 19:29; Deut. 23:17–18), fornication and adultery (Exod. 20:14; Lev. 20:10; Deut. 22:22; Ezek. 16:38–41; 23:43–49), and various other unchaste and impure acts (Exod. 22:19; 28:42; Lev. 15:18; 18:22–23; 20:13, 18; 18:19; Deut. 23:13–14; Ezek. 18:6; 22:10).

The sacredness of marriage comes to fullest expression in that it serves as an image of the covenant of fidelity between God and his people. Among other nations marriage was indeed brought into relationship with the deity, but in an entirely different way than in Israel. Paganism lost the concept of the holiness of God, turning the glory of the immortal God into the likeness of an image of mortal man and of birds and four-footed and creeping animals, and transferred to the deity the distinction of sexes, along with various immoral relationships and acts. Next to every male deity was a female deity that had relations with him, bringing forth children and living with him most of the time in discord and enmity. But all those immoral ideas are entirely foreign to Holy Scripture; the Hebrew language does not even have a word for a female deity. God is the Holy One and the Exalted One, who dwells in eternity; but he also dwells with those of a quiet and humble spirit; he keeps fellowship with his creature, and lives with his people in an intimate covenant. That covenant was entered into already with the patriarchs, but it was ceremoniously concluded and established with the nation of Israel for the first time at Mount Sinai. By virtue of that covenant Jehovah stands in a relationship toward Israel as with no other nation on earth. Jehovah is the rock from which Israel was hewn (Deut. 32:4, 18; Isa. 51:1),[2] the Father whom Israel denigrated (Deut. 32:6; Isa. 63:16; 64:8), the Husbandman who planted the vine of Israel (Isa. 5; Jer. 2:21), and more than that, was the Bridegroom and the Husband who had chosen and betrothed Israel to himself out of pure grace (Isa. 61:10; 62:5; Jer. 2:32; Ezek. 16; Hosea 1–3), and is now jealous of his honor, and regards all the apostasy of his people as harlotry and adultery, as sexual immorality and infidelity (Lev. 20:6; Num. 14:33; Ps. 73:27; Isa. 1:21; Jer. 3:1; Ezek. 16:32; etc.).

---

2 Ed. note: Original reads "Deuteronomy 33:4, 18 and Jeremiah 51:1" but is a typo.

5

THE FAMILY IN THE NEW TESTAMENT

The Holy Family

The New Testament opens with the story of the miraculous birth of Jesus from the virgin Mary. This fact is unparalleled in history. Among the pagan nations, various stories exist about sons conceived by the gods with women, but the birth of a child from a virgin who was overshadowed by the power of the Holy Spirit is entirely unique and without analogy. Mary occupies an entirely unique place in the history of the human race. She surpasses even the prophets and the apostles in esteem and honor; she alone was deigned to be mother of the Son of God; she is blessed and favored among women, and is called blessed by all the families of the earth.

And yet she was not saved by having carried Jesus in her womb and having nursed him at her breast, for those only are saved who hear God's word and keep it (Luke 11:27–28). And Mary did this.

When the angel brought her the message that moved her in the depths of her soul, she submitted herself completely: "Behold, I am the servant of the Lord; let it be to me according to your word!" [Luke 1:38]. Mary is the Israelitess par excellence, who does not run ahead and act on her own, but who receives in childlike faith what God bestows upon her. Whereas Eve detached herself from the word of God and went her own way, Mary accepted the word of God without murmuring or arguing; by God himself she was prepared and formed to be the receptor of his most sublime revelation. Just as in the beginning she did nothing but *surrender* herself in the fullest sense of that word to the will of the Lord, so too later she served as the mother who learned many wonderful things about her Son, but kept them with quiet pondering in her heart.

Before Mary received the angel's message, she had already been betrothed to Joseph, who was descended from the family of David and who practiced the carpenter's trade in Nazareth. The betrothal already had the character of a marriage relationship, although Joseph had not yet taken his betrothed wife into his own home. Before that happened, Mary was found to be pregnant by the Holy Spirit. Because Joseph knew nothing of the angel's message, and was a righteous man who desired to act according to the Lord's law in this matter, he harbored the intention of giving her a certificate of divorce and sending her away without scandal, merely in the presence of two witnesses. But an angel who appeared to him in a dream informed him of Mary's secret and told him not to be afraid to take Mary as his wife, for that which had been conceived within her was from the Holy Spirit. From that time on, Joseph never doubted for a moment the integrity of Mary's honor. He took her into his home as his wife and lived with her, but he did not know her until she had given birth to her firstborn son. It worked out under God's direction, according to the promise, and by means of the decree of the emperor Augustus, that the birth occurred not in Nazareth but in Bethlehem. Not only that, but it took some time before Joseph and Mary with the child returned to Nazareth. For in the first place, they stayed in Bethlehem until at least the thirty-one days were completed for Mary's purification and the infant could be presented to the Lord in the temple in Jerusalem. Secondly, the hostility of Herod and the slaughter of the infants in Bethlehem caused Joseph with the infant and his mother to flee by divine mandate to Egypt, and to return for the first time to Palestine and to Nazareth a couple years later after the death of Herod.

This explains why Jesus was known in Nazareth and the surrounding area simply as the son of Joseph and Mary. The parents kept the secret of his conception and did not mention it to any strangers. Only later, when Jesus showed by his words and deeds that he was the Son of God, and had acquired a multitude of disciples, did they likely mention it to several trusted friends. In this way, the wonderful story of Jesus' conception and birth was included in the gospel and made known to us in the books of Matthew and Luke. We learn nothing more about Joseph, however. When on a particular occasion the mother and brothers of Jesus look for him in order to talk with him and take him home with them, Joseph was not mentioned again. On the cross, Jesus commended his mother to the care of his disciple John. After the ascension only Mary, the mother of Jesus, and his brothers are mentioned. For all these reasons, it is not unlikely that Joseph died before the public ministry of Jesus began.

In this way, although he was the Son of God, Jesus was not ashamed to call Joseph his father, Mary his mother, and us his brothers. Just as during this entire period of humiliation he was obedient to the Father, so too in his obedience to his parents he sought to render obedience to his Father in heaven. It is explicitly stated that he was submissive to them and that he grew in grace with God and people [Luke 2:52]. The fifth commandment also belonged to that righteousness that he needed to fulfill as Savior of the world. True enough, for him spiritual kinship was more important than physical kinship. Even as Mary was not saved by the overshadowing of the Holy Spirit and the birth of Jesus, but by hearing and keeping God's word, so too Christ considered as his brother, his sister, and his mother only those who do the will of God (Mark 3:32–35). His earthly parents may therefore not interfere in those matters pertaining to his office and relating to his heavenly divine calling. When that happens, he resists even his own mother, not with a supercilious or deprecating tone but nonetheless strongly and decisively: as Son of the Father he is laboring in the business of his Father (Luke 2:49), and he alone decides concerning the hour when he will accomplish the work of the Father (John 2:4). All of that notwithstanding, submission to his parents also belonged to his mediatorial work. On the cross he forgets his own pain and thinks of his mother; with the most tender love he draws Mary's attention away from himself, gives her another son, John, the disciple he loved, and assigns to him the care of his mother (John 19:26–27).

Jesus' Regard for Women, Marriage, Parents, and Children

The holy family is the example of the Christian home. This example is strengthened by the words and deeds of Jesus. He himself was not married, for his bride is the church, whom he loved and for whom he gave himself so that he might purify and sanctify her [Eph. 5:26–27]. Nevertheless, he was not a monk who is too pious to look at and speak with a woman. Jesus dealt with women with complete openness and freedom; women were among his most beloved disciples; they follow him in Galilee and Judea, minister to him from their possessions, and are witnesses of his crucifixion and burial, of his resurrection and subsequent appearances. The disciples were surprised that he spoke with a woman in Sychar, but Jesus himself saw nothing strange about that, for everywhere and constantly and in everything it was his food to do the will of his Father and to complete his work (John 4:27, 34). With regard to the woman who in Simon's house had wet his feet with tears and dried them with the hair of her head, he forgave her many sins because she had loved much [Luke 7:36–50]. He allowed the adulterous woman to depart from him uncondemned, sending her away with the words: "Go, and from now on sin no more" [John 8:11].

Concerning the harlots and the tax collectors he says that they will enter the kingdom of heaven ahead of others. In this way Christ honored the woman and lifted her once again after her fall. At the same time he honors and restores marriage. Of course, there is no unconditional duty to enter marriage. There are circumstances in which one may be called to abstain from marriage for the sake of the kingdom of heaven (Matt. 19:12). There will come times of persecution when pregnant and nursing women will lament (Matt. 24:19). And marriage, despite being honorable and sacred, is a provisional state and is restricted to this earthly dispensation, for in the resurrection people will no more be taken or given in marriage; the redeemed will then be like the angels of God in heaven (Matt. 22:30). But within these boundaries, Christ acknowledged and respected marriage as an institution of God. Simply his attendance at the wedding in Cana and the first miracle that he performed there provide convincing proof of this. Moreover, he honored marriage especially when he traced it back to God's original ordinance and safeguarded marriage against various sins. Jesus did not come to give a new law, including in relation to marriage, but he came to fulfill the law and the prophets and to bring them to full realization and application [Matt. 5:17–20]. So when he explains the seventh commandment in the Sermon on the Mount, he forbids not only the sin of adultery, but he says that one who even looks lustfully at a (married) woman has already committed adultery with her in his heart [Matt. 5:27–28]. Such a person, if it were up to him, would already have caused that married woman to commit adultery and have broken up her marriage. But not only may no one break apart the marriage of another, but neither may he destroy his own marriage. Moses did indeed permit a husband to give his wife a certificate of divorce and send her away; but that permission was due to the hardness of hearts and was not grounded in God's original ordinance; it was lawful but not moral, permitted by the court but not in the conscience.

Among Jesus' disciples, then, matters should proceed differently. Anyone who divorces his wife to marry another not only commits adultery himself, but causes the divorced woman to commit adultery, as well as the one who takes her in marriage (Matt. 5:32; 19:9). Sin gives birth to sin; adultery destroys not one, but several homes. Jesus permits divorce in one case; in Israel a married woman did not have the right to divorce her husband, although the husband could divorce his lawful wife; yet if a married woman was guilty of sexual immorality and thereby in fact broke the marriage, then the husband *did not have to* nor was he *obligated to* divorce his wife, but he *may* do so, and with a free conscience he may release his unfaithful wife and view the marriage as having been in fact dissolved. With this Jesus did not intend to supply a ground for divorce that was supposed to be legally valid and was supposed to be included in the law. Concerning that he says nothing at all. He does not say what the lawgiver in this or that country must stipulate with regard to divorce. But he supplies a *moral* law that must bind the conscience of his disciples. In connection with that, he proceeds from the original institution of marriage. In terms of its nature and essence, marriage is the bond of one man and one woman becoming one flesh for their entire lives. In this way God has joined them together, and what God has thus joined, man may not put asunder (Matt. 19:4–6).

Added to this is the great love that Jesus showed to children. The kingdom of heaven surpasses everything in value; for the sake of the gospel everything must be left behind—house and field, brothers and sisters, father and mother, wife and children. Whoever loves father or mother, son or daughter, more than him is not worthy of him (Matt. 10:37). But beyond this constitution of the kingdom, Jesus establishes the bond between husband and wife and just as importantly, between parents and children, as once again something unbreakable. The Jews always had the custom of making various misguided and superficial vows whereby they bound themselves, if this or that danger were averted or some benefit or other were received, to set aside a gift for the temple and for religious purposes. The rabbis did not oppose this wicked custom, but sought to regulate it so that such a promise, once made, could be honored and fulfilled in agreement with the law (Deut. 23:21–23). Occasionally this went so far that those vows were kept at the cost of moral obligations that children have toward their parents. And this is what Jesus was opposing (Matt. 15:4–6; Mark 7:10–12). If someone says: "That which I could have used for the support of my parents is Corban, which means, I have vowed to donate it for the temple," and if the scribes then say that such a vow may not be broken for the sake of the honor due to one's parents, then by their entire interpretation they are ensuring that a child can do nothing more for his father or mother. At that point the command of God is rendered powerless by means of human regulations.

Just as here Jesus is restoring in general the force of the fifth commandment, so too several times elsewhere he shows that he has a profound understanding of the tender relationship that exists between parents and children. He sympathizes with the lonely epileptic and mute child whom a man from the crowd brought to him, and he healed the child from his sickness (Matt. 17:14–20). He saves the child of the royal official from death (John 4:46–54), was moved with inner pity concerning the widow in Nain who was bringing her only son to the cemetery, whom he called back to life (Luke 7:11–15), and a little while later raised the little daughter of Jairus from the dead (Luke 8:41–56). Jesus loved children with a grand and profound love. He permitted the children to come directly to him and laid his hand on them in blessing (Matt. 19:13–15). He puts them before his disciples as an example of simplicity, uprightness, and humility (Matt. 18:3), and he rejoices about the little ones who believe in his name (Matt. 18:5). Even as on the day of his royal entry into Jerusalem the children in the temple shouted their hosannas to him, he views that as fulfilling the Old Testament idea that from the mouths of young children and nursing babies the Lord establishes strength and fashions praise for himself (Matt. 21:16).

The Apostolic Teaching

The entire instruction of the apostles agrees with these words of Christ. It is already remarkable that all of them, like the brothers of the Lord, with the exception of Paul, were likely married, including Peter as well (Matt. 8:14; 1 Cor. 9:5[1]). Like Jesus, Paul considered the unmarried state in some instances to deserve preference (1 Cor. 7:1–17), but he is a far cry on that account from disapproving marriage as impermissible or marital relations as impure. On the contrary, in opposition toward those who command abstaining from marriage and from various foods, he insists that every creature of God is good and nothing is to be rejected if it is received with thanksgiving and consecrated by the Word and prayer (1 Tim. 4:3–5). Marriage is not only honorable (Heb. 13:4), but already from the time of its institution it was, and in terms of its essence continues to be, a symbol of the intimate fellowship existing between Christ and his church. Earthly marriage images the heavenly, and serves to prepare for this heavenly marriage; for the ultimate goal of history is that a humanity may emerge of which Christ is the Head and in which God is all in all (Eph. 5:32).

Marriage is therefore not a Christian institution in the sense that it owes its origin and its arrangement to Christianity. For it dates from the creation, having received at that time its rule and law, and despite the frequency of its corruption, appears among all peoples. The New Testament as well returns repeatedly to the original institution of marriage to derive from that the regulation in terms of which marriage should be arranged today. Adam was made first, then Eve; the man is the head and the glory of God, but the woman is the glory of the man; man was not created from woman but woman from man; and Adam was not tempted, but the woman was tempted and fell into transgression. On all of these considerations is based the admonition that the wife must acknowledge the husband and support him as head of the family (1 Cor. 11:7–9; 1 Tim. 2:12–14). The ordinance whose basis lies in creation is neither weakened nor destroyed by special revelation. Rather, it is established and strengthened thereby, and acquires a richer and deeper significance through special revelation.

---

1 Ed. note: Original reads "2 Corinthians 9:5" but is a typo.

If marriage images the fellowship between Christ and his church, then this ought to be manifested primarily in that fact that both husband and wife enter their marital covenant in the Lord (1 Cor. 7:39). In general the apostle warns believers not to be yoked with unbelievers (2 Cor. 6:14). He is not wanting thereby to cut off all contact with pagans, for then Christians would actually need to get out of the world (1 Cor. 5:10; 10:27). Rather it is undoubtedly his intention that believers should not enter into such fellowship with unbelievers whereby they are robbed of their own freedom, become unfaithful to their Christian duty, and could be brought under the yoke of unbelievers. Even though Paul is speaking there in general terms, nevertheless it is not impermissible to apply his word to mixed marriage. For such a marriage entails the serious danger that the believing spouse will settle for something in life that conflicts with the kingship of Christ. And that may not happen; even if one spouse is converted to Christ and the other remains an unbeliever, as occurred frequently in Paul's day, then the Christian spouse ought to set the tone. That spouse's home ought to be a Christian home, where the unbelieving husband is sanctified through the believing wife and the children are holy as well (1 Cor. 7:14).

For a Christian family is a family in the Lord, a family in fellowship with Christ, according to his example and command, in the unity of his Spirit. The confession of Christ does not destroy the natural order; the husband remains the husband, the wife remains the wife, and children remain children, even as the slave who is converted to the Lord does not thereby cease being a slave. But the relationships of husband and wife, and of parents and children, although corrupted and destroyed by sin, are nevertheless restored and renewed by Christ. So the husband remains the head of the family, since he is the image and glory of God, and the wife remains submissive to him, because as one created after and from and for him she is the glory of her husband. Nevertheless, how wonderfully their mutual relationship is renewed and sanctified! In Christ there is no man and woman (Gal. 3:28), both are heirs of the grace of life (1 Peter 3:7), both share the same faith, the same baptism, the same Lord's Supper, both have received the same Holy Spirit, both share the same access to the Father.

Even though the natural distinction and the original relationship between husband and wife continue to exist, everything nonetheless acquires a different character; the husband must love his wife, live for her, and surrender himself to her, even as Christ loved the church and gave himself up for her, while the wife must be in submission to her husband in the Lord and as unto the Lord (Eph. 5:22–33; Col. 3:18–19; 1 Peter 3:1–7). Similarly, children continue to be obligated according to the commandment to render obedience to their parents (Eph. 6:1–3); both parties do not stand in opposition against each other, but they constitute a unified fellowship in the Lord; likewise, the children are holy, ought to be at home in the domain of the church, and are heirs of the promise of the covenant (Acts 2:39; 1 Cor. 7:14; 1 Tim. 2:15). Parents must nurture their children in the teaching and admonition of the Lord, and children must love their parents and obey them in the Lord (Eph. 6:1, 4; Col. 3:20–21). With all their differences, husbands, wives, and children together constitute a chosen generation, a holy people, a royal priesthood (1 Peter 2:9).

Finally, if marriage is such an intimate communion of husband and wife that it may be called a symbol of the unity of Christ and his church, then it is obvious that it can be nothing else than a bond between one man and one woman entered into for the rest of their lives, dissolved only by death. Even as Christ, so too Paul says that each husband shall love his own wife (1 Cor. 7:2; Eph. 5:31, 33), that especially the elder and the deacon may not live in fellowship with more than one wife (1 Tim. 3:2, 12;[2] Titus 1:6), and that those two shall become one flesh (Eph. 5:31; 1 Cor. 6:16). Such a bond endures until death. Even difference in religion that arises with the transition of one spouse to Christianity does not dissolve the marriage; a spouse who has become a believer may

---

2 Ed. note: Original reads "1 Timothy 3:2, 22" but verse 22 is a typo.

not abandon his or her other half (1 Cor. 7:12–14), and if this situation has occurred contrary to the command of God, then the spouse who divorced must either remain unmarried or return and be reconciled with his or her other half (1 Cor. 7:11). If, however, the spouse who has remained an unbeliever had obtained the divorce, then the blame for that rests with that spouse, and the believing spouse cannot be compelled to reestablish the broken bond (1 Cor. 7:15). Whether this believing spouse who was abandoned by his or her other half through no fault of their own may enter another marriage is not answered by Paul. He was satisfied simply with pointing out that the believing spouse may never dissolve the marriage.

The Blessing of Christianity for Family Living

By means of all these prescriptions and instructions, Christianity has been a rich blessing for family living. Among the ancient Romans marriage was held in high honor, and the housewife occupied a very prominent place in family life. But when Greek and Oriental customs penetrated Roman society, and wealth and prosperity led to the disappearance of its former simplicity, a moral deterioration gradually arose that in the days of Paul, given his description in Romans 1:26–32, had achieved terrible proportions. Marriage existed often merely as a mutually acceptable temporary cohabitation; divorces were the order of the day. When men did not avoid marriage altogether out of indolence, and did not seek the satisfaction of their lusts in other ways, nevertheless in practice a man was not devoted to one wife, but maintained relations with harlots and concubines, thereby pushing the lawful wife more and more into the background. The number of children was arbitrarily limited; for their nurture children were entrusted to the slaves, and there was hardly any evidence, at least in various circles of society, of a family life between husband and wife, between parents and children. Along with all these evils came the so-called unnatural sins as well, whereby the natural relationship with one's wife was exchanged for an act contrary to nature, and men committed shameful acts with men. At times it seemed as if the days before the flood and the abominations of Sodom and Gomorrah had returned.

The confession of Christ made its appearance in this immoral society at that time. One may not forget that at first it frequently brought great division into the homes. Christ had not come to bring peace to earth, but a sword, and to put a man at variance with his father, a daughter against her mother, a daughter-in-law against her mother-in-law. The earliest history of the Christian church provides many examples of this; husband and wife, father and son, mother and daughter, brothers and sisters often came to stand in opposition against each other as enemies on account of the faith, and many who embraced Christianity had to leave everything to be worthy of Christ and to be his disciple. What it must have cost Perpetua[3] to resist the pressure, the supplications, and the tears of her father and to remain faithful to her confession!

But in the face of all of this, we find that the Christian faith brought peace to many a heart and returned love to many a home. Christianity did not overthrow the natural ordinances and institutions, but infused a new spirit in them, reforming them from within. It did not liberate wives from their husbands, or children from their parents, or servants from their masters, or workers from their vocations, or subjects from the state. But Christianity made for better wives and children, manservants and maidservants, workers and citizens, and led them back to their respective relationships. Christianity provided spiritual liberation, and precisely in that way recreated earthly relationships. One who was called as a servant remained a servant, but became a freeman of the Lord; and one who was called as a freeman became a bondservant of

---

[3] Ed. note: Perpetua was arrested with some companions, perhaps most notably Felicitas, and, after some time in prison and despite the pleading of her father to renounce the name of Christian, she suffered martyrdom with her companions as part of the gladiatorial games, most likely in Carthage in the year 202, during the reign of Septimius Severus.

Christ (1 Cor. 7:22). Precisely through this preaching of obedience and love Christianity performed miracles.

From the beginning Christianity found entrance especially among women. Not only was Jesus accompanied by various women during his travels in Galilee and Judea, but after his ascension they gathered with the apostles and with them received the gift of the Holy Spirit. In the church established by the apostles or their fellow workers, women appeared repeatedly as prominent members who played an important role. We are told about the many women who belonged to the church in Jerusalem (Acts 1:14; 5:14), not only Mary the mother of Jesus, but also Mary the mother of Mark (Acts 12:12). While we are told concerning Thessalonica and Berea that many prominent women there were converted to the Lord (Acts 17:4, 12[4]), the book of Acts and the letters of the apostles acquaint us with Tabitha in Joppa, with Lydia in Philippi, with Damaris in Athens, with Priscilla in Ephesus, with Phoebe in Cenchreae, with Nympha in Colossae, and with Euodia and Synteche in Philippi. And in Romans 16 Paul mentions, in addition to eighteen brothers, no fewer than eight sisters to whom he was sending his special greeting.

Many of these women also performed significant ministries in the church; they received [the apostles] in their homes (Acts 12:12; 1 Cor. 16:19; Col. 4:15), helped the apostles in the work of the ministry (Rom. 16:3, 6–15), occasionally led in the gathering of believers, though not to teach (1 Cor. 14:34; 1 Tim. 2:12; 1 Peter 3:1), but certainly to pray and to prophesy (1 Cor. 11:5), and were perhaps occasionally tasked with one or another project in the midst of the congregation, without holding a particular office (Rom. 16:1; 1 Tim. 3:11; 5:3–16). From a later period we know that the preaching of the gospel found entrance among the women as well, and they themselves worked for the spread of the gospel; they often surpassed the men in studying the Scriptures and in the knowledge of the truth; they matched the men in terms of deeds

---

4   Ed. note: Original reads "Acts 17:4, 20" but verse 20 is a typo.

of faith; many suffered martyrdom for confessing Christ and were held in high esteem by the church and were frequently admired by pagans.

This spiritual elevation of the woman benefited the home as well. It may be truthfully stated that Christianity brought to light once again the beauty and the richness of the life of the soul of the woman. Christianity did exclude the woman from ecclesiastical office and did not elevate her to the rank of a priestess, but it did introduce a universal priesthood of believers in which the woman shared as well, and did so in no small measure. The significance that the woman acquired in the church affected her position in society. Whereas in the Roman world she was gradually denigrated to the position of slave or an instrument of pleasure for the man, now with Christianity she again became a unique, independent personality with her own mind and will. She remained man's helpmeet, but along with him inherited the same grace. In the Christian faith, husband and wife were restored to one another, and various sins of harlotry and unchastity, adultery and divorce, had to give way to the love that bound both of them together anew. Christianity sanctified marriage, liberated it from various evils, and once again established it on the foundation of the divine commandment.

Just as Christianity bound husband and wife together again, so too it gave parents back to their children, and children to their parents. The wife became mother once again in the true sense of the word, the one who not only gives birth to her children but who also nurtures them. And children obtained rights as well, such as the right not to be destroyed before birth and not to be killed or abandoned as a castaway after birth. In the corrupt society there were actually no longer any fathers and mothers, any spouses and children. But now they were all once again bound together in one circle and in one family; and that family was not merely a part of the state, but it acquired an independent existence and became the foundation of the entire civil society.

DANGERS CONFRONTING THE FAMILY

The Ascetic Movement within the Christian Church

It is hardly the case that the principles proclaimed by Christ and the apostles for marriage and family have found full and pure application in all times and places. Christianity often gets blamed for not having been able, across the span of eighteen centuries, to redeem society from all its evils, from poverty, greed, prostitution, etc. Such a complaint leads people to lose sight of the fact that the human person always remains the same and continues to be born with the same wicked heart. From that heart proceed evil thoughts, murder, adultery, harlotry, thievery, false witness, and blasphemy [Matt. 15:19]. As soon as these evils spot an opportunity, they break forth and spread throughout all of society. In this dispensation, therefore, complete victory is never achieved and complete rest never obtained. From generation to generation and from century to century, the struggle against sin must be continued, and the spiritual and moral nurture must begin afresh with each person.

For that reason, it is not enough to know and confess good principles; they must be developed and applied continuously, day after day, moment by moment. As soon as slackening occurs in this application, the enemy exalts himself and once again assumes mastery over the lost territory. The history of the family within Christianity is therefore a story not only of the incalculably rich blessing deriving from the Christian confession for family life, but also of various aberrations and evils that have appeared repeatedly in this area and that served to undermine and destroy marital life.

To the latter belongs the ascetic movement that soon became manifest among many Christians.[1] Different causes supplied entrance to the idea that abstaining from various natural things, from food and drink, from rest and relaxation, and especially from marriage, was a God-pleasing and highly meritorious endeavor. The Christian church never erred to the extent of condemning marriage and family life as such; but the church did go so far as to confess that abstaining from these earthly concerns was a shorter and safer path to heavenly salvation. Marriage and the unmarried state were not related to each other, as Augustine said, like sickness and health, but certainly like temporal health and eternal immortality. Married life might be silver, according to the formulation of Chrysostom, but the unmarried state is golden.

This ascetic movement led gradually to hermitic living and monasticism. These arrangements may not be condemned unconditionally, for monasticism was a rich blessing for the spread of Christianity, for the work of mercy, and for preserving and advancing civilization. In addition, Jesus speaks emphatically about such

---

[1] Ed. note: Bavinck is critical of all forms of Christian piety, whether they be intentional or inadvertent, that led to devaluation of the married state, the importance of marriage and family life, and the family's role as a primary cultural institution. But he sometimes overstates this point.

people who abstain from marriage and sexual relations for the sake of the kingdom of heaven, and Paul declares that for an unmarried person it is good—i.e., morally permissible—not to touch a woman, and that the unmarried are preoccupied with the things of the Lord while the married are preoccupied with the things of the world. Voluntary abstinence is not only permitted, but in special cases and for specific purposes can even be obligatory. But the ascetic movement that arose in the Christian church gradually began to harbor the notion that the unmarried state in itself was always better than marriage, and that it was a meritorious work to commit oneself by an unbreakable vow to lifelong celibacy. In so doing, the ascetic movement departed from the instruction of Christ and the apostles, which never included approval of such meritoriousness of the unmarried state and of such a lifelong vow.

This unofficial pressure on people's consciences often had the most terrible repercussions. One may fully acknowledge the gains achieved by monasticism with respect to Christianity and civilization, without closing one's eye to the deeply immoral situations it caused, which especially in the centuries preceding the Reformation had reached a frightening level and had expanded in every Christian country. The church forgot the word of the apostle Paul, that it is better to marry than to burn, and that each has received his own gift from God, the one this gift and the other that gift [1 Cor. 7:1–9].

The church especially forgot this with respect to the spiritual class. For although most of the apostles, including Peter, were married, and though among the apostles in the early Christian church marriage was the rule, nevertheless the idea gained currency that the administration of spiritual things was incompatible with marriage and family life. The new ethics arose especially with Pope Gregory VII in service to the hierarchy of the Roman Catholic Church. If the church was to remain independent from subservience to the laity, from the powers of the world, and from domination by the state, then before anything else its spiritual class needed to be separated from women, from marriage, from the family, from offspring, and it must be dependent only on the church. In this way the interests of the hierarchy pushed for the unmarried state for the spiritual class, and undoubtedly enjoyed the benefits of that. But the yoke that this placed on the conscience of Roman Catholic priests was unspeakably heavy.

Rome and the Reformation

The same idea led the Roman Catholic Church to elevate marriage to a sacrament. It appears to be a direct contradiction that on the one hand, marriage was forbidden for the spiritual class, and on the other hand, that marriage nonetheless bore the character of a means of grace. But both notions proceed from the same consideration; they are two branches growing on the same tree. Taken by itself and viewed strictly as a natural phenomenon, marriage is not much more than a fleshly communion unworthy of the Christian, or in any case something belonging to a much lower order than the state to which one is elevated by faith. If marriage were to be permitted for the Christian and were to be maintained, however, then it should be elevated through supernatural grace to the status believers themselves have now achieved.

And that is the idea being expressed by Rome in its understanding of marriage as a sacrament. As it was instituted at creation and as it still currently exists outside the Roman Catholic Church, marriage is nothing but a "natural" communion of husband and wife. But through his merits, Christ has perfected this earthly marriage, and sanctified it, and elevated it to be an instrument of his supernatural grace, just like baptism and the Eucharist. If marriage is lawfully entered, before the altar by the priest in the presence of at least two witnesses, in the name of the Father, Son, and Holy Spirit, then the marriage partners share in a supernatural grace that equips them not only to live together in unity and love, but also to bring forth and nurture children to propagate the human race and the church of Christ at the same time.

For Rome, the Christian sacredness of marriage does not consist in marriage being inwardly renewed, freed from sin, and purified through the Word of God and prayer. Rather, its sacredness lies in this, that to natural marriage, which though not particularly sinful and impure still belongs to a lower rank and bears a profane character, is added and bestowed a supernatural grace. The Christian element does not saturate the natural, but continues to hover above the natural. The natural is not renewed by grace but only suppressed; the bridle is laid upon the desire that properly belongs to the flesh by nature, but the flesh itself is never renewed; the leaven is indeed sprinkled over the dough, but never kneaded within so that the dough becomes saturated with it.

The correctness of this observation is proven by the deprecating language with which numerous Christian writers often expressed themselves in former centuries with regard to marriage and women. When scholars argued whether the woman could be called a human being, then this was mainly a linguistic issue, whether the masculine word for "man" applied to the woman. But positing the question already betrayed a perspective of the woman as being less valuable than the man. And such a perspective reappeared among the most extraordinary men in early and later centuries. The Jewish rabbi Meir recommended that a man offer three prayers of thanksgiving each day, the first that God did not create him a Gentile, the second that God did not create him a woman, and the third that God did not create him a fool. In the same way Christian men often considered themselves to be elevated high above women. Often among the church fathers the counsel was given not to eat, drink, and speak with women, but to flee from a woman's path as from the gaze of a serpent. Men saw the woman to be primarily a temptress of the man, a snare unto sin, a "gateway of the devil," as Tertullian called her; and with all these accusations men forgot to seek the guilt in their own weaknesses. The apex of this despising of women was reached in the famous book of two Dominican monks that appeared in 1487 under the title *Hammer of the Witches (De Malleus Maleficarum)*. Because it considered the woman far more susceptible than the man to demonic influences, the book spurred the intense persecution and burning of witches.

Despising the woman did not lead, however, as one could momentarily suppose, to abstinence, but to abuse. If marriage was denigrated, if the woman was viewed as inferior to the man, and if marital relations were thought to be impure, then all of this has but one result: satisfaction of lust was sought outside of marriage and the woman was abused as an instrument of pleasure. Asceticism, as it came to be united with religion, sooner or later brought to life the reaction of libertinism; when nature is suppressed for a long time, it soon enforces its rights in response, and casts off every constraint. During the Middle Ages, especially since the tenth century, the denigration of women was accompanied by prostitution. Liberated women traveled throughout the countryside or settled in the cities to form a kind of guild, all in order to sacrifice honor for the sake of lust. Dissoluteness knew no limits in the palaces of kings and nobles and in the dwellings of prosperous citizens. Literature and art turned their back upon medieval barbarity in response to greater familiarity with Greek antiquity, and frequently became serviceable to the glorification of the natural man. A man like Boccaccio, for example, contributed in no small measure to the decay of morals by his novel *The Decameron*. Members of the spiritual and monastic classes were swept along in large numbers by the same currents of impurity.

At that point the Reformation did stem the tide somewhat. Especially the strong moral reformation that arose in Geneva under Calvin's leadership and from there gained entrance into various countries, generated a beautiful series of household and civic virtues that later in our own country found their passionate poet and eulogist in Cats.[2] In addition, however, the destructive powers continued to have an effect. The free spirits gladly seized the

---

[2] Ed. note: The reference here is to Jacob Cats (1577–1660). His book *Marriage* (1625) focused on women and contained chapters on the six stages of a woman's life.

opportunity to trample underfoot not only ecclesiastical tradition but also every regulation of religion and morality, and to proclaim the gospel of the liberation of the flesh. Naturally, the divisions and wars that were afflicting the nations during the sixteenth and seventeenth centuries strongly fortified the indifference of heart and the degeneration of morals. Later when peace and rest descended and prosperity increased through business and industriousness, people who lived in the palaces of princes and in the homes of aristocrats surrendered to various kinds of excess and hedonism. The immorality of the French royalty set the tone for many countries, and together with increasing unbelief, prepared the way for the great Revolution. Rousseau was its spiritual father; and as the preacher of an unbound religion of feeling, he himself lived with concubines and abandoned his children. In the French Revolution the public women played a prominent role and marriage was robbed of its Christian and sacred character.

The Sexual Problem and Attempted Solutions

Prostitution has existed throughout time and among every nation, and it seems that nothing is able to eradicate it. But in the nineteenth century for various reasons it acquired an unusually grievous character and obtained a frightening growth. In the first place, intellectual anarchy contributed in no small measure to the increase in immorality. For when the sense of religion diminishes, the notion of good and evil is erased, the sense of responsibility and guilt is suppressed, so that passion and lust have free rein and the wickedness of the heart breaks forth openly in the form of shameless evil acts. To this was added, in the second place, the refinement of entertainment and pleasures that was advanced by the exaggerated value placed on material goods, all of which aroused among many people antipathy toward marriage and toward the burdens of a family. Finally, the social situations today are often of such a nature that they prevent many young men and women from getting married, and induce them to seek the satisfaction of their needs in a sinful manner. Wealth and prosperity as well as poverty and misery pave the path of disgrace. And that path is broad, and many there are who walk upon it.

In previous centuries prostitutes constituted a relatively small group, but today in the large cities their multitude numbers in the thousands and tens of thousands. This situation is all the more frightening because it is the cause of various venereal diseases that are spread in society, transmitted from husband to wife, from parents to children, putting at risk the health of families and generations, indeed, of the entire populace. It is these diseases that, as they crawl about in secret, undermine the physical well-being of many people, causing hidden suffering that is never talked about, accounting for a high percentage of the mentally ill, blind, deaf-mutes, and deformed, such that society ends up bearing even heavier burdens. From every side, therefore, the investigation and study of sexual issues is being discussed. What is to be done to resist the cancer of sexual sin that gnaws on the body of the human race? What is its cause and what means can be used to fight against it? Naturally the answers to this complex issue range far and wide. No unanimity exists regarding either the cause, the nature, or the treatment of this abysmal evil.

There are some who expect all help or at least the most help to come from regulating prostitution. They proceed from the assumption that prostitution has existed in all times and places, and that it is ineradicable. It may well be an evil, nevertheless it has in any case appeared to be a necessary evil. Stop, they implore us, with the futile attempt to eradicate this evil. Rather, accept it and acquiesce to it. And seek to liberate prostitution as much as possible from the deleterious consequences that often flow from it. Make it safe, subject it to oversight and regulation by the state, engraft it into the social organism, give the brothel a charter and the prostitute a license. People need to stop viewing prostitution as a sin to be opposed, and see it much more as a sickness that requires the attention of the medical health industry.

Dangers Confronting the Family

Alongside them others come forward who also want to place marriage more and more under the regulation of the state. They view it as irresponsible that anyone, even if they suffer from a hideous and incurable disease, may get married, have children, and procreate. In their opinion, for that reason in the future marriage should be subject to the care of the state, and be made serviceable to the propagation of a strong generation. Artificial breeding, which until now has yielded favorable results with plants and animals, will in the future also be used with people. Today lawmakers have determined the age and kinship requirements for marriage; let them continue along this path by obligating everyone wanting to get married to undergo a medical test, and in some specific cases even by prohibiting a particular marriage, thereby to further the salvaging and strengthening of the human race!

In direct opposition to this stand those who assign the cause of all misery in sexual conduct to the ancient institution of marriage.

They cannot find words sharp enough to condemn this institution and all the legislation of church and state regarding this matter. No institution can ever be good, so they reason, that binds two people to each other for their entire lives by the marital bond, compelling them to live together even when passion has disappeared and love has been displaced by coldness, which in addition subjects the wife to the caprice and lust of the husband. Liberation must be the watchword! The state and the church must retreat entirely from this arena; no law, no rule, no bond, no impediment pertaining to marriage any longer! Let the entire business be left to human inclinations! Let them unite together freely, according to passion and whimsy, in love. Perhaps then, as some expect, freedom will gradually achieve what compulsion cannot acquire. Love will bind many until death. But if that should not be the case, then it is better to divorce than to be forced to live together. If free marriage cannot bring about an enduring union, then allow free love to live as it prevailed at the beginning of the human race! Children provide no obstacle to this ideal, for if no other arrangement is suitable, let them be taken care of by the state!

Still others expect all deliverance to arise from the emancipation of the woman. In former times the woman was always a toy or a slave of the man. She could never develop herself freely and independently according to her nature. This explains why after centuries of oppression in various respects she now lags behind the man, in physical strength, in intellectual capacity, and in scientific prowess. But all of that will change when the woman becomes completely independent of the man in and outside of marriage, and when she is viewed and treated as an equal. Let every profession and job, every position and office be opened to women. People have opened for her not only the door of the classroom so she can teach, and the corridors of the hospital so she can show mercy. Now let them open for her the colleges and universities, the pulpits and lecterns, the judicial benches and the council chambers. Let her be given suffrage in the state, the church, and in various organizations! Then women will show what they can do; they themselves will provide for their own livelihood or be forced into the sin of prostitution. Through their unique feminine virtues they will provide a counterbalance to the coarseness and ambition of men, and in family, society, and state they will demonstrate a reforming, salutary power.

Finally, there are also those who cast the blame for all sin and misery on the lousy organization of society, and within that society, especially on capitalism and the unequal distribution of goods. Poverty is the cause of every malady, of prostitution and drunkenness, of robbery and murder. If society were organized differently, suddenly an end would come to all those miseries. Suppose society were organized in such a way that everyone would enjoy rest and relaxation at the appropriate time, in such a way that everyone received from the public treasury an equal wage or a subsidy equal to their needs, then the reason for all envy and hatred, for all sin and wickedness, would disappear. People would live together like brothers and sisters; complete equality would be the guarantor of harmonious brotherhood. The freedom of individuals and of families would indeed suffer some damage; perhaps parents would have to hand over their children soon after birth to the state for communal education. But the equality and fraternity are well worth this small sacrifice of freedom!

In this way there is no lack of proposed remedies for the maladies of modern society. But the remedies being proposed are for the most part just as damaging for marriage and family life as the maladies. There has never been a time when the family faced so severe a crisis as the time in which we are now living. Many are not satisfied with remodeling; they want to tear things down to the foundation.

7

MARRIAGE AND FAMILY

Reformation in Terms of Christian Principles

All good, enduring reformation begins with ourselves and takes its starting point in one's own heart and life. If family life is indeed being threatened from all sides today, then there is nothing better for each person to be doing than immediately to begin reforming within one's own circle and begin to rebuff with the facts themselves the sharp criticisms that are being registered nowadays against marriage and family. Such a reformation immediately has this in its favor, that it would lose no time and would not need to wait for anything. Anyone seeking deliverance from the state must travel the lengthy route of forming a political party, having meetings, referendums, parliamentary debates, and civil legislation, and it is still unknown whether with all that activity he will achieve any success. But reforming from within can be undertaken by each person at every moment, and be advanced without impediment.

A still greater advantage accrues to the internal, spiritual-moral reformation in that it does not conflict with nature. Most changes currently being proposed to solve the sexual problem not only contradict Christian principles but also come into conflict with the facts and demands of reality. Open marriage and free love, the emancipation of the woman, and the socializing of society, fail to take into account reality whether it be sound or sick. They all suffer from the illusion that by means of external measures, by means of abolishing old laws or implementing new laws, they can change human nature or convert the wicked human heart. They all travel the route from outward to inward, thinking that a person, whom they view as a product of circumstances, will be gradually renewed in a different environment.

In comparing these modern attempts at reform to that reformation recommended and implemented by Christianity, we are filled with an ever-deepening amazement about the latter. For in a manner that cannot be surpassed, Moses and the prophets, Christ and the apostles, have distinguished between reality that is safe and that which is sick. In other religious and philosophical systems, both of these spheres are always confused or blended. But the special revelation that comes to us in Christ sharply distinguishes them; though it acknowledges nature, comprehensively and fully, it nonetheless battles against sin across the entire spectrum of reality. Everywhere and always it seeks the reformation of natural life, but only in such a way and by such means that nature is liberated from unrighteousness. Christ came simply to destroy the works of the devil, indeed, but with the further goal of bringing the works of the Father once again to manifestation and honor along that route.

This explains why Scripture proceeds from the distinction between man and woman. This distinction was neither a human discovery or invention, nor a product of circumstances, nor the result of a slow and gradual evolution, but has existed from the very beginning, provided by nature itself and consequently called into existence by God, who placed it before our eyes as an undeniable fact. With John Stuart Mill we can indeed say that the woman's nature is not an immutable phenomenon, but was formed gradually by the oppression committed against her, or we can fantasize with others that the original human being was a sexless or an androgynous being.[1] But then we would be reasoning quite apart from reality. Culture can surely bring about some changes, but it can do so only within specific limits and on the foundation of nature itself. People and nations were very different from each other in various times and circumstances, but the man has always been a man and the woman has always been a woman. There is nothing mutable about this fact; we have only to accept it. It is not a work of the devil to be destroyed, but a work of the Father to be acknowledged.

The Distinction between Man and Woman

Nevertheless, we can both underestimate and overestimate this distinction. The first defect often hobbled people in previous centuries. In practice people frequently viewed the woman as a being

---

1 Ed. note: Perhaps the earliest source of this idea is pre-Christian: Aristophanes's speech in Plato's *Symposium* 189c–193e, though hermaphroditic might be more accurate than androgynous. Aristophanes claims that originally humanity had three genders, one all male, one all female, and one hermaphroditic or androgynous, originating from the sun, earth, and moon, respectively. Eventually Zeus splits each of them in two out of anger and now each person is looking for his or her "missing half." The all-male halves look for other males, the all-female for other females, and only those who were once part of the hermaphroditic or androgynous sex seek heterosexual relationships, their missing halves being of the opposite sex. It is unclear whether or not this speech is meant for comic relief or serious consideration. Nevertheless, some early Gnostics embraced the idea that humanity was originally androgynous. An analogous view can be found in the Jewish Kabbalah as *Adam Kadmon* or the original, primal man. Similar conceptions have enjoyed notable popularity in the modern period in Germany through such figures as the early Lutheran Jakob Böhme (1575–1624), the writer Johann Wolfgang von Goethe (1749–1832), the Roman Catholic philosopher and mystic Franz Xaver von Baader (1765–1841), and the Romantic Karl Wilhelm Friedrich Schlegel (1772–1829), among others. It is likely that Bavinck has these or similar figures in mind. This idea, often associated with Genesis 1:27, still retains some popularity today. For an English translation of Plato's *Symposium*, see Plato, *Symposium*, trans. Benjamin Jowett (Upper Saddle River, NJ: Prentice Hall, 1956).

of lower order than the man, and theoretically people often denied her the status of being fully human. Over against that view, we must maintain, with the help of Scripture which alone supplies an explanation regarding the origin and essence of a human being, that both man and woman are created in God's image, and that therefore both are human beings in the fullest sense of the term. The second chapter of Genesis presents the woman especially as a helper suitable for the man, but let us not forget that this chapter has been preceded by the first chapter of Genesis. Here we read that God created man and woman together in his image; the woman can be a helper suitable for the man only because she is his equal and reflects God's image just as much as he does. The question that has been raised upon occasion in the past, namely, whether the woman may be called a human being, is not at all appropriate. The woman is a human being no less than the man, because she no less than he was created in God's image. Scripture speaks in a very human way about the essence of God, but it never transfers the sexual differentiation to him; God is never portrayed or presented as being feminine. But if the woman is said to be created along with man in the image of God, then that includes the fact that the uniqueness and richness of feminine qualities no less than those of the masculine capacities find their origin and example in the divine Being. God is a Father who takes pity on his children, but he also comforts like a mother comforts her son.

Because of this unity of human nature, then, the well-known saying is not entirely true that claims that the man is incomplete and half a person without the woman, and the woman without the man. It is true only insofar as each is viewed separately in his or her own particularity. But the expression is less correct when one thinks of human nature, which is common to both. Each of the two is complete as a person. Man and woman each have a soul and a body, a mind and a will, a heart and a conscience, a spirit and a personality. There is no single capacity of the body and no single quality of the soul that is exclusively unique either to the man or to the woman. Each of the two has a fully human nature and is a uniquely independent personality. For that reason, the question is so difficult to answer as to whether the woman possesses less of an aptitude for some activities and functions than the man. For although understanding and rationality, head and hand, undoubtedly function in a different way with the woman than with the man, that does not at all imply either a different or an inferior aptitude, and is not at all identical to inability.

Related to this is the difficulty of describing crisply and clearly the distinction between man and woman. Judgments span a wide range, and it requires no artistry to arrange alongside one another the contradictory opinions of those with profound understanding of human nature. Down through the centuries and among all nations, among philosophers and among the unreflective masses, women haters have exchanged places with women worshippers. And men have hardly remained constant in their own judgment, but frequently move from the one to the other extreme. At one time or another, the woman is an angel or a devil, a queen or a vixen, a dove or a serpent, a rose or a thorn. The feminine is identified as divine, and then again as demonic. The man kneels before her in worship, only then to pin her under his foot. Frequently the conclusion is that the woman is a riddle; the man does not understand her, and yet he often understands her even better than she knows herself.

Nevertheless, the distinction exists, and it is set in terms of its main features as well. There is outward difference between man and woman, in terms of the body and all of its organs. Difference in the size of the head, in the development and weight of the brain, in the tint of the skin, in the growth of hair, in the shape of breast and stomach, in the form of the hands and feet. Difference also with regard to the strength and tone of the muscles, the sensitivity of the nervous system, the gracefulness of movements, the color of the blood, the flow of tears, the pulse rate, the sound of the voice, the multiplicity of needs, the capacity to suffer, the weight and strength of the body. In her entire development, the woman is closer to the child and reaches full adulthood sooner than the man.

No less important is the distinction between man and woman that exists in the life of the soul. People have said that the soul has no sexual differentiation, but even though the nature and capacities of the soul are the same for man and woman, they function in a different way. By means of observation the woman acquires sense impressions more quickly and retains them longer and more deeply than the man. Her imagination is characterized by greater liveliness and quicker connectivity. Her thinking and evaluating are characteristically more visual than analytic, attaching more value to the amenities of life than to abstract principles and rules. She seeks truth preferably along the route of an idealizing view of reality, rather than by the method of conceptual analysis. With the man, the volitional capacity is more logical, more capable of persistence, more persevering in striving for a goal, but the woman surpasses him in forbearance and patience, in the capacities for suffering and adapting.

The human nature given to man and woman is one and the same, but in each of them it exists in a unique way. And this distinction functions in all of life and in all kinds of activity. Already the outward appearance of the woman makes an entirely different impression than that of the man, and has an entirely different significance for her than for him. Clothes and jewelry are less important for the man, but with the woman they are an important part of her life. For that reason people often call women "the fairer sex." That entails no insult, as long as it does not intend to portray the masculine sex as "the ugly sex." For just as the description of women as "the weaker sex" [1 Peter 3:7] does not imply that all forms of weakness are combined in the woman, similarly the description of women as "the fairer sex" does not imply that all beauty has been bestowed on the woman. The man is beautiful as well. Only an unhealthy school of thought relating to beauty and art acknowledges no higher beauty than that of a naked female body, time and again abusing her in various seductive and hideous poses as though she were nothing more than an ornament.

Such an unhealthy school of thought also entails that people no longer have an eye for the beauty of the man. Yet, such beauty exists as well. It is a different beauty, quite surely, but of no less value. It is the beauty of loftiness that the man embodies, even as the beauty of comeliness is the possession of the woman. But both man and woman are beautiful; both display the features of the image of God in which they are created. To the man belongs the strength of physical prowess, the wide chest, the commanding eye, the full beard, the powerful voice; to the woman belongs a delicate shape, sensitive skin, full bosom, round shape, soft voice, long hair, elegant carriage, and supple movement. He engenders respect, she engenders tenderness. In terms of beauty, Michelangelo's *Moses* is not inferior to Raphael's *Madonna*.

Similarly, the woman is constructed differently than the man in terms of religion, intellect, and morality. The same laws of logic and morals, the same religion and morality apply to both. The man is not intellectually superior to the woman, and the woman is not morally superior to the man. But how entirely different each of them takes hold of religion and morality, art and science! The man sees in religion first of all a duty, the woman considers it a pleasure and a privilege. For the man, the good functions more in the form of justice, for the woman it takes the shape of love. The man wants justice and law, the woman sympathy and participation. The man strives for the truth of an idea, the woman pursues the reality of life.

Accordingly, each must be on guard for a particular set of sins. The man must struggle against forcing his principles and pressing upon others every possible consequence, and the woman must wrestle continually against her deficiency in logic that is manifested both in rigid tenacity and incorrigible willfulness, as well as in a fickleness that defies every form of argument. The man is susceptible to the danger of doubt and unbelief, rationalism and dead orthodoxy, while the woman risks no less a danger of superficial piety and superstition, mysticism and fanaticism. The loquaciousness of the woman contrasts with the incommunicativeness of the man. The vanity of the woman is no worse than the coarse indifference of the man. The infidelity of the man is matched by the stubbornness of the woman. Indeed, man and woman have nothing to hold against each other. Each has quite glorious virtues and each has rather serious defects. There is room for neither disparagement nor deification with respect to either of them.

The Unmarried State

The uniquenesses of man and woman, therefore, make the one indispensable for the other. Each of them is in their own way incomplete, not as a human being but as a man or as a woman. The man finds in the woman his complement and his corrective, and conversely, the woman finds in the man the very same things. Without the woman, the man easily becomes insensitive, dissolute, egocentric, and without the man the gentleness of the woman degenerates very easily into weakness, her love into sentimentality. Just as she cannot dispense with his independence and strength, he cannot be without her dependence and tenderness. Marriage is thus grounded in the nature of both. Human beings did not invent marriage, nor was marriage introduced by the state, nor imposed by the church, but it was provided along with human nature and instituted by God himself with the creation. "It is not good that the man should be alone" [Gen. 2:18], God said in the beginning, and therefore it *is* and *remains* so. For this reason Holy Scripture knows of no *prohibition* against marriage, a proscription for anybody, for any priest or prophet, for any apostle or teacher. Scripture condemns those who forbid marriage and in this respect, Scripture is directly opposed to every kind of asceticism. Material reality, the body, and sexual differentiations are all of divine origin. The woman did not originate after the fall, but was created as woman along with the man, in true knowledge, righteousness, and holiness in the image of God [Col. 3:10; Eph. 4:24]. In Holy Scripture there is no *prohibition against*, but only a *command for* marriage.

But like all other moral commandments, this command, which in this manner is established in general and is to be protected against all human ordinances, is nevertheless given to rational people and thus requires a rational application. It is not good for a person to be alone, to be sure, but that in no way entails that a person may marry carelessly. God himself restricts the implementation of his command by means of age, monogamy, and various degrees of kinship, all of which limit marriage. God also restricts marriage by the gift of abstinence, a particular calling that he occasionally entrusts to people. Jesus himself was unmarried and speaks of such people who assume for themselves the obligation of abstinence for the sake of the kingdom of heaven [Matt. 19:12]. And Paul says that there can be circumstances in which it can be better for someone to remain as he himself was.

So one cannot and may not say that for everyone marriage is always an indispensable condition for reaching one's destiny. Just as marriage usually leads to having children, and a childless marriage is not for that reason without benefit and purpose, so too it is the usual path for an adult man or woman to get married, but if someone sees the route to marriage blocked, they are not for that reason missing their destiny. Such a view would indeed be shared by everyone who confines the destiny of a person to this life, to the propagation of the race, to sensuality. But those who stand on the foundation of Christianity and believe in the eternal destiny of people cannot and may not hold such a view. A man and a woman are human beings before they are husband or wife. Marriage does not belong to the essence of being human. Although unmarried, Jesus was a genuine and complete human being, and without any defect he completed the work that the Father had given him to do. Numerous men and women have abstained from marriage and devoted themselves with all their strength to missions and mercy, to science and art, and gave themselves in most valuable service to humanity. In heaven people will no longer be married or be given in marriage. Marriage is thus a temporary, provisional institution, and within marriage fruitfulness is limited to a part of life.

One may not say, therefore, that someone misses their destiny if they cannot enter marriage. Neither may we defend the kind of preaching that declares marriage to be necessary for every person with a view to a person's sensual nature. In their day, the Reformers placed heavy emphasis on this in response to the immorality prevailing everywhere among the spiritual class and in the monasteries. In so doing, they did nothing different than what Paul declared, that because of unchastity each man should have his own wife and each woman her own husband, and that it is better to marry than to burn. Only prudishness can blind the eyes to the immense power of sensuality.

Still, one must guard against overemphasis on the other side by saying that marriage is necessary for everyone. For then one easily risks the danger of drawing the conclusion that someone who has no opportunity to get married may satisfy his desires in another manner. Years ago numerous doctors agreed in their opinion that such satisfying for young men was obligatory or at least permissible with a view to their health. But later, powerful voices arose against such license to commit sin. Today numerous medical experts acknowledge that abstinence is neither damaging to a person's health in the least nor impossible to practice. Moreover, preaching the absolute necessity of marriage robs a person in advance of the weapons he needs to fight against his passion. It weakens rather than strengthens him; it induces him to give up in the struggle before he begins; it surrenders the fort before the enemy even launches the attack.

A person can, however, certainly be called to wage such a struggle. History, especially modern history, yields innumerable examples of that. Jesus demanded that people leave all for his sake, needing to hate and even lose one's own life for his sake; in the administration of his providence God often calls many men and women to deny themselves when it comes to marriage, and to crucify the flesh with its desires. He assigns to people the duty of performing their vocation and pursuing their life purpose not through marriage but outside of marriage. Surely the cross that he places on their shoulders is heavy. People not called to such self-denial often make it worse by heaping insults upon unmarried people and selecting them to be the object of their bitter scorn.

But God knows that suffering as well, mixes it with his compassion, and makes it bearable in the power of faith. The mistake of the Roman Catholic Church lay, then, not in making room for celibacy alongside marriage; it would have been much more desirable if Protestantism could have found some room for celibacy. But its mistake consisted in this, that it considered the unmarried state, along with the vow of obedience and poverty, to be a faster and safer route toward perfection, and thereby drew numerous men and women away from family life, people who would have been more suited for that and been a far richer blessing there. For marriage is no less honorable than celibacy, and in itself it is not any more difficult and longer route toward perfection. Which of these routes is the best for a person and must be taken by a person depends only on the person, or rather on the calling of God that a person feels in his heart, and the decision thus rests with a person's conscience. No state and no church has the right to violate this conscience by means of its own self-initiated ordinances.

Marriage As the Norm

Nevertheless, even though celibacy can be permissible and obligatory in particular circumstances, for man and woman marriage is still the usual route along which they perform their calling and work toward their improvement here on earth. As a rule it does not depend on a person's choice whether they will marry or not. Each person is driven by their own nature. From the time when self-awareness is awakened, the distinction between the sexes gradually becomes part of that awareness and with increasing measure gains attention and occupies the thoughts of the heart; it occupies half of people's thinking, feeling, and acting.

No matter in what remarkable stages this development of sexual life may occur, it moves in one direction, it constantly demonstrates the character of a unique, incomparable inclination, and finds rest for the first time in the full fellowship of marriage.

No time is as remarkable as that when love awakens and expands across all of life. Poets have sung about it, sages have thought about it, art and literature derive their richest motifs from it, and the heart of every person is full of it. The blossoming of the rose in the garden, the appearance of spring in the course of the seasons, the rising of the sun in nature are no more beautiful than the opening of the human heart to the luxuriousness of love. From the hidden depths of the life of the soul rises a world of stirring beauty. Sentiment overpowers the senses, driving back every other impulse and surpassing all others in intimacy and power. Experiences are enjoyed that are not to be compared with any other in tenderness and depth. Ideals are formed, for which all the richness of life contributes material. Expectations for the future are cherished, the kind that reach far above the wildest dreams. On all these experiences marriage sets the crown. It is the apex of human life, the ultimate goal of years of effort, the victory after a long struggle, the destination of a long preparation. When the groom brings the bride to his home, then love celebrates its most beautiful triumph, while heaven and earth lift up their song of blessing.

At this point the novels usually end their stories; at least that is what they used to do in a more idealistic age. Today, now that realism has taken over in art, harboring the illusion that it sees and understands reality better than the romantics, people take pleasure in describing life after the wedding and in marriage, presenting it as one huge disappointment, as an intolerable cohabitation, as a desperate situation of misery and duress. Poetry is then introduced into this situation by means of sinful passions, forbidden affection, unnatural lust; these are glorified and smothered with glitter at the cost of love and fidelity in marriage. Poets, artists, novelists, and playwrights compete with each other in denigrating marriage and in surrendering to the hostility of the public. In thousands of hearts they stifle faith in the ideal and extinguish pure and virtuous love.

There is one element of truth in this school of art: after the wedding, the seriousness of living gets underway for the first time.

Once the couple "have each other," then for the first time begins the test as to whether they will keep each other. If earlier romanticism was blind to this, it was just as guilty of imbalance as the newer art, which also envisions reality merely from one side and just as narrowly. For to be sure, there are many unhappy marriages, more than we might suppose or know. There are people by the thousands bound to each other for life who are more a curse than a blessing to one another, and who in their marriages are already living a hell on earth. When the best gets corrupted, it becomes the worst; love that wanes becomes hatred, and affection that dissipates gives way to aversion. When marriage loses its delight, it turns into unbearable drudgery.

No difference of sentiment can exist regarding these facts; they are too numerous and they speak too loudly. But in attempting reformation, one can proceed in either of two directions. One can attempt to justify those facts and defend them as normal, and then all blame falls on the institution of marriage, and the person in such a marriage who commits harlotry and adultery goes free, and for his dissolute passion receives a crown on his head. Then divorce, open marriage, and free love are the solution to the problem. Then science and art, lectern and stage, must cooperate in undermining and overthrowing existing marriage.

But people can also be convinced that this cure, though recommended in the name of reality and science, of beauty and poetry, is worse than the disease. This conviction finds support in the conscience of every person. In the modern era, as the notion of sin is slipping away, the culpability for every misery is being sought outside the person and located in the institutions, in social circumstances, in the organization of the state. All deliverance is naturally expected then from social and political reform. But conscience speaks a different language within every person who seriously examines himself and ventures to confront this moral reality. Such a conscience lays the blame not on the institutions of society and state, but on the person himself; you are the man! That is how the prophets and apostles spoke; this was the teaching and example of

Christ: just like the entire moral law, marriage is wise and holy and good, being of divine origin and rich in blessing for the human race, but human beings have invented many schemes.

The Choice of Spouse and Courtship

They invent such schemes already before marriage, in the choice of a spouse. Let us leave out of consideration those who already before marriage have lapped up lust like water and entered marriage with an impure heart and often with an unchaste body! What must and can be expected from a marriage that long beforehand was defiled by various sins, entered after one's best strength has been spent, and entered only on the basis of calculation? But if we renounce these abusers of the good and of the sweetness of marriage, what superficiality and frivolousness are exposed with the choice of a spouse! In ancient times entering into marriage was the business of the parents, the family, and the tribe; the search for a spouse was initiated by the parents, and it was directed by the parents (Gen. 24:20; 28:1; 34:11; 38:6). This situation ran the risk that parents failed to take into account the inclination of their sons and daughters, and exercised domination over their heart and hand already during their adolescence. Today, however, sons and daughters have often become so independent and wise that they hardly bother any more with the wishes and advice of their parents or friends, and frequently proceed in the opposite direction. To an often momentary passion all other interests are sacrificed.

With the choosing of a spouse it must be remembered first of all that marriage is a *moral* institution. It was not invented by us nor is it regulated by us; it exists by virtue of God's ordinance and includes its own law and rule; in this sense it is laid upon us from above and from outside of us, and we need to answer the question how we ourselves will enter marriage in accordance with those divine laws. In terms of this resolve we are bound on every side; we are bound by the parents from whom we are born, by the family of which we are members, by the social circle in which we live, by the village or city where we dwell, by the vocation we practice, by the church to which we belong, by the confession we have made, by the capacity we have acquired, by the path of life we have chosen. For that reason, entering marriage is not a question of the choice of free will where one seeks the advice of his own fancy and desire. We must take into account all the circumstances in which God has placed us, and from those we must deduce what he has to say to us.

For that reason it was absolutely correct when former interpreters of the moral law emphasized that in choosing a spouse, one should take all these circumstances into consideration and reflect upon the leading of God's providence in them. Certainly great significance may be attached to the affection of the heart, as long as it is genuine and not merely a flush of infatuation; but such affection does not exclude taking into account one's confession and personal piety, age and status, health and suitability. In sum, according to the admonition of the apostle, a Christian may marry only in the Lord, that is to say, in fellowship with, according to the will and with the approval of Christ, who is our only Master and Lord. The young man and young lady who have committed themselves to each other must be able to thank the Lord uprightly for bringing them together. That is the proper marriage in which the husband confesses about his wife, and the wife about her husband: I did not choose him or her by means of my understanding, but God granted him or her to me. He has led this man, this woman to me as though with his own hand.

Then, after the initial commitment comes the glorious time of engagement. Engagement is far more than what is expressed by the phrase "going steady." This phrase actually refers to bargaining for someone's hand, the attempt to obtain someone's favor by means of civilities, and thus lends to such favor the character of a triumph achieved through struggle, a prize that must be won in a contest. The commitment of the woman, which binds her to the marriage, also bears this character. The shyness that is unique to her, the reservedness behind which she retreats, is not an unnatural self-control, not a learned "art of modesty," as Cats commends it,[2] but the natural protection of innocence and an invaluable guarantee for an honorable engagement. For in our country this is characterized on the one hand, by a freedom of concourse, such as would otherwise be unimaginable and impossible between a young man and a young woman, and on the other hand, by a restriction of freedom that calls for patience and self-control. Engagement is the forecourt to the sanctuary; it supplies a sacred right and at the same time imposes an enduring duty. Although it is surely better if, during this time of preparation, they must break up by mutual consent and for good reasons, for it is better to turn back after going halfway rather than to travel all the way by mistake. Nevertheless, it is irresponsible the way in which many young men before or during the time of engagement play with the girl's heart like they're playing with dice.

Engagement corresponds to its purpose only when it prepares for the fellowship of marriage. It is absolutely not simply an opportunity to get to know each other's virtues, but just as much, and perhaps even more importantly, it is a laboratory for beginning to learn to tolerate one another's faults. It brings into balance both the expectations of marriage and the disillusionments from marriage. When two people are going to unite with each other for life, then they must not imagine that it will always be roses and sunshine, without a cloud in the sky, no thorn growing along life's pathway. Those who do not know the sin of the human heart, indeed, the sin of their own heart, can easily surrender to such an illusion. But the Christian ought to be on guard for that, also during the engagement, for he knows better from the testimony of Scripture and from his own experience. The engagement confirms this truth; it helps the young man and the young woman understand ahead of

---

2 Ed. note: The reference here is to Jacob Cats (1577–1660). His book *Marriage* (1625) focused on women and contained chapters on the six stages of a woman's life.

time that marriage will be not only a gift, but also a task, not only a privilege, but also a calling.

One who has learned this during the time of engagement is prepared for both the blessing and the burden of marriage. For such a person, the multiform adversity and cross mentioned in one Reformed liturgical marriage formulary are not a discordant note to his ears. People can differ about whether these risks ought to be mentioned at such an early stage; but that they belong in the liturgical formulary cannot be disputed. They express the healthy realism of Scripture in opposition to the unhealthy realism that is being expressed in contemporary literature and art.[3] Reality remains the same, but everything depends on the eye through which it is viewed. Modern realists view the risks of marriage as the results and fruits of this institution itself, and for that reason they rebel against it and curse marriage. The Christian sees adversities and crosses in marriage, which overcome us on account of sin, and accepts them as a means to exercise one's faith. No Christian says that the person is corrupted by marriage, but he confesses that marriage is corrupted by the person; the modern realist blames the circumstances, the institutions, the laws and ordinances, ultimately, God himself, while the Christian finds within his own heart the source of all impurity.

---

3 Ed. note: The Form for the Solemnization of Marriage first appeared in a 1566 edition of the Dutch Psalter edited by Petrus Dathenus (1531–88), a leading minister in the Reformed churches in the Netherlands. In composing this, and other liturgical forms, Dathenus borrowed heavily from existing liturgies based on Calvin's Geneva liturgy. The Reformed churches adopted these forms at the Convent of Wesel in 1568. The likely passage on weathering adversity in marriage that Bavinck alludes to above is as follows: "Although it is true, as the apostle says, that those who marry will face trouble in this state and because of sin will experience many difficulties, yet they may also believe the promise of God that they, as heirs of the grace of life, will always receive His aid and protection, even when they least expect it." English translation taken from the Form for the Solemnization of Marriage of the Canadian and American Reformed Churches.

Sins to which Husband and Wife Are Exposed in Married Life

To those adversities and crosses that overcome those who are married belong not only the various risks of life, disaster and accident, sickness and death, need and misery. But to these belong also the faults and sins that married people need to put up with in one another. Often husband and wife are each other's cross. And if the wife is not the husband's cross, or the husband the wife's cross, that he or she must carry, then each has one or another quality that is a disappointment or an irritation to the other. Who has ever found a husband or a wife who corresponds entirely to the other's expectation or corresponds fully with the ideal that one had formed in his imagination? In marriage the virtues find an especially favorable opportunity to unfold and be developed; but the faults and weaknesses are also nowhere more clearly exposed to the light as in the intimate circle of the family. Many a husband, who appears great and strong in the eyes of other people, is weak in his home, petty and narrow-minded; and many a wife, who seems like an angel when she is visiting others, in her own home is a pest to her husband. Who shall comprehend such wandering in marital life and in the sphere of the family? And who shall count the sins committed so often by husband and wife against each other?

In this connection Scripture is the only book that speaks the truth and sees reality clearly. It sees reality far better and is far more prepared to tackle it than is the most powerful artistic realism. But it proceeds entirely differently, for it does not call out to those who are married: "Continue walking on the path of sin; pay no attention to any law or rule." But rather, Scripture holds accountable those who are married, grips them in their consciences, and calls them back to the law and to the testimony. To the husband and the wife, to each of them, Scripture directs a particular and a serious admonition.

The great sin to which the husband is exposed in marriage is *infidelity*. The honeymoon period is soon past, and when the wedding dress and veil are put away, so too the beautiful illusions. With many, love gives way to coldness, coldness to indifference, indifference to neglect. And the husband who once swore to his love with the most precious of vows, seeks diversion and the satisfaction of his desire in a bar or a club, and with another woman; brothels are patronized mostly by married men. Knowing this danger, Scripture emphatically and repeatedly addresses the husbands: You husband, love your wife; do not become embittered with her; dwell with her with understanding and give her the honor that befits her as the weaker vessel. For this, Scripture points the husband to no one less than Christ himself as the example. Entirely voluntarily, out of the fullness of his authority, he loved the church, which in herself possessed nothing lovable; he loved her with an eternal, unchanging love; he loved her with a total denial of himself, at the cost of his own self, all the way to death (Eph. 5:25–30; Col. 3:19; 1 Peter 3:7).

As long as the husband is not loving his wife according to this example, with voluntary, unswerving, self-sacrificial love, he has nothing to demand from her, as long as he has not kept the law. Only this is love in the truest sense of the word—to love for the sake of Christ, willingly and freely, faithfully and unswervingly, all the way to death. But such love does not remain without fruit. Christ loved his church, and he acquired and won her by the power of his love. He purifies her and presents her as a church without spot or wrinkle. The husband who loves his wife according to this example will gain and win her, will raise her to his height, and will treat her as his equal. For no wife can resist that kind of love. But even if that should not happen, the husband will through his royally open love nevertheless register this costly gain, that his prayers will not be hindered (1 Peter 3:7). One who travels the forbidden path and pursues forbidden fruit can no longer pray. He can no longer pray at mealtime and he can no longer pray in solitude. He might still mumble a few sentences for a time, but he is no longer praying. His praying is no longer coming from his heart and therefore no longer reaches up into heaven; it is soulless and dead, it dies on his lips and finds no way up. In the bordello people don't pray, they only curse.

The great sin to which the wife is so easily liable and against which she must struggle, is *stubbornness*. The consent of the wife signifies that she declares herself to have been gained and won, that she is giving herself in the fullest sense to the man of her choosing. But this promise contains more and is more difficult to keep than many a wife thinks at the outset of marriage. It requires immense, continual self-denial, and she easily comes to think that the wishes and demands of her husband are unfair and unreasonable. This danger threatens especially when the husband is chosen not out of love, but for the sake of his status or office, or worse yet, if the woman enters marriage in order thereby to acquire a position within society. Then the husband is almost ranked after the housekeeping, the children, furnishings and clothes, the glamor of the salon, and the yearning to please others. Even though outwardly the form is still preserved, inwardly the distancing has already occurred, and she withholds from him everything pertaining to her soul and body over which she has power, and drives her husband further and further away, to the path of sin and shame.

Seeing this danger, Scripture opposes such a wife, calling her back from her excesses, and holding before her this admonition: You wife, be submissive to your own husband; remember that the man is the image and glory of God, that he was made first and the woman was created from him and for him, that not he, but the wife was the first to transgress, and that the wife must be obedient to the husband, as to the Lord Christ, and as it is fitting in him (1 Cor. 11:3–9; Eph. 5:22–23; Col. 3:18; 1 Tim. 2:12–15).

This admonition is fortified with a twofold addition; the first is this, that the wife must show obedience to the husband so that the Word of God might not be blasphemed on account of her (Titus 2:5). For the same Word prescribing obedience for the wife also commands obedience from children toward their parents, from the servant toward his master, from the maid toward her mistress, from the citizen toward his government. If the wife is disobedient toward this Word of God, then she is setting a bad example for her children and servants, and she is also provoking them to disobedience. This evil works its way out from the small sphere of the family throughout society and the state, and undermines the foundations of both. The other addition points out that the wives who in accordance with the command of the Lord are submissive to their own husbands, will perhaps by their behavior win these husbands to the Lord, men who through the preaching of the Word were not brought to faith (1 Peter 3:1). When the husbands see the power of the Word in the life of their wives, then they too will surrender to that Word and glorify the name of God.

The Subjection of Husband and Wife to the Command of God

The human heart always opposes these admonitions of Holy Scripture. Especially at the present time we see powerful opposition against these ordinances of God. The husband refuses to honor the command to love, saying that he cannot love a wife who has so many faults as he sees in her. The wife refuses to be obedient to a husband who is so unreasonable in his demands and so tyrannical as she has come to know him. Both exert pressure for multiplying and easing the opportunities for divorce. The demand is sounded continually louder and stronger that open marriage and free love might be enjoyed, or at least that the laws for marriage might be radically changed. "We need to get rid of the idea that the wife must follow and obey her husband, and that divorce can occur only in special cases, particularly those mentioned." Thousands upon thousands already live as though there existed no law regulating marriage. They live together in an open relationship with the man or woman of their desire; they hardly bother themselves about the command that the husband must love his own wife and the wife must obey her own husband; and they even lie to the judge, and the one charges the other or allows oneself to be charged with the crime of adultery in order to be able to get divorced and enter an impermissible relationship with someone else.

Now, we are not dealing here with the legislation of the state regarding marriage. Perhaps just like the Lord himself did among Israel, the lawmaker will need to take into some account the hardness of the human heart. Scripture is not a law code that lies ready to hand for the government. But this much is certain, that the same Scripture proceeds from an entirely different understanding and prescribes an entirely different pattern of conduct. It does not call the husband to continue down the path of his sinful appetites and passions, but to stop and turn back. If you do continue down that path, Scripture says, then you will bring about your own destruction; you will destroy your family, fracture the required nurturing, corrupt society, undermine the state; along that route lies no rest and no peace, but only death and judgment. Conversely, if you abandon this path and begin again to live according to God's commandment, if the husband once again loves his wife and the wife is once again obedient to her husband, then unity and peace and love will return, then the marriage will be established, the family renewed, the wife restored in her honor, society reformed, the state reborn. From the family outward, blessing and prosperity will once again spread across all the nation.

One can reject this instruction of Scripture, but one thing cannot be contradicted, namely, if husbands and wives walked according to this rule, they would enjoy marriages and family life that would surpass every earthly association and community in beauty and radiance. One must not allege against Scripture the objection that it prescribes for the husband a sugary, insipid love that condones everything about his wife, and that Scripture assigns to the wife an obedience that would make her little more than her husband's slave. For in the first place, Scripture addresses those who understand its message, not those who abuse it. Secondly, those who talk this way betray that they understand the essence of neither love nor obedience. Genuine obedience includes righteousness, and genuine obedience is the demonstration of freedom.

Thirdly, Scripture declares that the love of the husband for his wife, and the obedience of the wife toward her husband, must be shown "in the Lord," and "as is fitting in the Lord" [Col. 3:18]. In so doing, Scripture gives an example of the depth and power that must characterize love and obedience, but also indicates the boundaries within which both must be shown. Both have their example, but at the same time their measure, in God's covenant with his people, in the relationship of Christ toward his church. They are not absolute, but relative and conditional; they are not the highest, but subordinate to the highest. Therefore Christ, who condemns divorce as strongly as possible, can nevertheless demand that one forsake husband or wife, parents or children, house or field for his sake, and follow him. Within marriage as well, one must obey God rather than people; consequently, the husband's love and the wife's obedience are limited to the things that are right and fair. In fact, marital communion is the highest, the most intimate, the most tender that can be imagined between people. Such a communion presupposes the mutual independence and freedom of personality. Only within marriage does the personality of husband and wife, and of each according to their natures, come fully into its own.

For that purpose marriage was instituted in the first place, so that they might help "each other faithfully in all things that belong to this life and to the life to come."[4] Even if marriage is not blessed with children, it can still satisfy this purpose. Before children are born, the marriage is already a fellowship of life, and remains so until death, even after the children are grown and have left their parental home. The essence of marriage lies in the full and complete communion of husband and wife, with body and soul together, for all of life. For that reason it is monogamous, the bond of one man and one woman. Polygamy denigrates the woman into an object of sensual lust and corrupts the family. Such a complete

---

4 Ed. note: See the Form for the Solemnization of Marriage of the Canadian and Reformed Churches referenced in the previous note.

union as marriage is, wherein two people become one soul and one flesh, cannot be anything but monogamous. The love of the husband for his wife and the obedience of the wife toward her husband are incapable of being shared. In terms of this depth and comprehensiveness, this intimacy, power, and duration, the fellowship of marriage is to be distinguished from every other fellowship among people, from every friendship and affection, from every cooperative and association.

It finds its example and likeness only in God's covenant with his people, in the communion of Christ with his church. Already at its beginning, marriage is such a full and complete fellowship; but if it is the genuine article, it increases daily in fellowship. The benefit that God has bestowed upon the children of men with the gift of marriage is constantly sensed more deeply and savored more richly. At the beginning one doesn't realize even a fraction of this; but as time progresses, and the years multiply, among the adventures and disappointments of life, the souls of husband and wife grow together more intimately, until marriage comes to be acknowledged more and more as the most precious and priceless gift of God on this sinful, thorn-covered earth, and the estate of marriage becomes a cause for worship and gratitude.

How then can people speak of marriage as a contract that can be terminated and broken at any moment? In its essence and according to its nature, it is just as unbreakable as the bond between a mother and her child. It is the most intimate, the most profound, the most tender love that binds husband and wife, from every side, for their entire lives; it is a moral institution that nurtures, enriches, and perfects both husband and wife. Church and state neither invented nor instituted marriage; they can only validate it before God and before people. Marriage itself is of divine origin; he established the law for marriage, a law that binds every person, as well as the church and the state; he created it as a reflection of that most intimate fellowship that he in Christ enjoys with his church. And he has destined it as a sacred estate, wherein people nurture and prepare each other for the kingdom of God.

8

FAMILY AND NURTURE

Sexuality

Marriage establishes a bond first of all between husband and wife, so that they may help and support one another in all things belonging to temporal and eternal life. But in the second place, another purpose is to propagate the human race and to expand the kingdom of God. With the institution of marriage, therefore, God immediately pronounced the blessing of fruitfulness. God created human beings from the beginning as man and woman, so that they might multiply and in this way fill the earth and subdue it. Sexual difference and sexual relations therefore rest in God's arrangement and are acceptable to him.

Through this idea about the origin and purpose of marriage, Holy Scripture cuts off all asceticism at its root. In this context we are to understand that school of thought that ascribes great inherent moral value to abstaining from various natural things, like food, drink, marriage, sexual relations, etc., and considers this abstinence a more direct and safe way to perfection than being preoccupied with various earthly concerns. It always proceeds from a stronger or weaker dualism, that is, from a certain opposition between spirit and matter, and is guided by the idea that matter, if it is not particularly sinful, is nonetheless inherently unclean, something profane, something belonging to a lower order.

But Scripture proceeds from another principle; it teaches that the earth no less than heaven was created by God, and that matter, soul, and body are all of divine origin and therefore are not inherently unclean. They can be unclean only through sin, but then not only matter and the flesh, but also the spirit; or rather the spirit in the first place, since sin is a moral phenomenon and lodges first in the soul, in the human will. But apart from sin, nothing is inherently unclean; every creature of God is good, and nothing is to be rejected, but to be received with thanksgiving [1 Tim. 4:4].

Therefore Scripture often speaks so simply and openly about matters involving sexuality. Scripture neither elaborates on this nor goes into detail, and it certainly does not revel in its descriptions of sexuality, unlike modern literature and art repeatedly do. But Scripture also lacks every kind of prudishness, every façade of decency, every bit of hypocritical modesty; when things happen, Scripture calls them by their name. It adopts a posture of healthy realism and is not improperly called the Book of Love—love in its fullest and richest sense, a love that binds all creatures together, and, having been disrupted by sin, that is restored by divine love.

But on the other hand, Scripture also avoids libertinism, that is, every form of striving to make the flesh independent from and higher than the spirit. When for a time asceticism gains the upper hand in religion and morality, in literature and art, sooner or later another school of thought always arises that glorifies natural life and moves easily to the other extreme. At that point, sexuality is not merely restored to its rightful place, but often it is loosened from all moral restraints. People hoist the slogan of the emancipation of the flesh and indulge every desire. The sexual urge is elevated to the noblest of all human desires, the sexual organs are viewed as the focal point of the irrepressible will to live, human seed is honored as the quintessence of all power, and procreation is glorified as the only genuine sacrament, as the most holy activity, as the highest deliverance. So exalted and sovereign are sexual relations viewed that they need not be governed by any law and may be freed from all conventional restraints.

It requires little argument to show that Holy Scripture directly opposes this licentious sexual living. In various ways sexual relations are given restraints, by means of natural aversion embedded in the conscience of every human being, by means of degrees of kinship within which marriage is forbidden, by means of limiting fertility to particular years within the span of human life, by means of monogamy that permits the bond between one man and one woman alone, by means of the seventh commandment that in principle governs the entire life of marriage. For this commandment teaches us that all unchastity is accursed by God and for that reason, we must despise it from the heart and live chastely and modestly, whether in the holy estate of marriage or outside of marriage. In the New Testament this commandment is impressed upon believers even more strongly by reminding them that their bodies are members of Christ, destined for the resurrection, and temples of the Holy Spirit. With this holiness, in which not only the soul but also the body participates, all harlotry, all unchastity in word and gesture, in thought and desire are in perpetual conflict. Marriage is entirely and wholly a sacred institution of God, and within marriage sexual relations are also bound to the moral law.

Procreation, Unity, and Diversity in the Family

The lofty moral significance of procreation also comes to expression in the fact that it bestows existence upon a human being. An ecstasy of desire is joined with the most sublime solemnity. For if one ponders that a moment of passion bestows existence to a person, who from the moment of his or her conception is subject to sin and death, with the birth a life emerges into the world filled with trouble and sorrow, and continues to exist endlessly, then every joke dies on our lips and our heart is filled with profound respect for this mystery of life. For it is and remains a mystery, despite all scientific research. What the poet sang regarding the miraculous way in which he was made in secret and was designed with artistic craftsmanship in the lowest parts of the earth, that is still the culmination of all wisdom [Ps. 139:13–16].

The origin and essence of life are hidden, the origin of the soul with all its power is hidden, the effective activity proceeding from the father and the mother is hidden, the cause of fertility and infertility is hidden, and the reason for the correspondence and differentiation between parents and children, and among children themselves, is hidden. The entire area of inherited traits remains one immense riddle. With procreation the persons involved are mere instruments; through them, a higher, creative power is working. God is the One who creates people through the instrumentality of people, and who places them each with a special individuality on the stage of this world. Equally mysterious as the love that husband and wife bring to one another and that unites them to each other is the power that causes children to be born from their union, children who display one predominant type and yet are different from each other in various respects.

But through this creating power God's artistic work comes into existence bearing the name of home and family. By itself this is immediately of predominant importance, namely, that every person, before leaving his father and mother and cleaving to his wife at a point later in life, has lived for years in the family and was born from that community. From your earliest existence, from the moment of your conception, you are the fruit of communion and exist only in and through such community.[1] That community did not come into existence through your will, but existed already long before you, gave you life, nurtured and sustained you. It is a community of mem-

---

[1] Ed. note: In Dutch the word *gemeenschap* is used to refer to both to communion and community.

bers, of parents and children, of brothers and sisters, who belong together and live together by divine will, and in which we are members and participants apart from any consent on our part, by virtue of the same divine will. We do not choose them, nor do they choose us; we can do nothing by way of adding to or subtracting from the members; whether we later find it agreeable or disagreeable, we can change nothing about it. Our lineage, our ancestors and parents, our brothers and sisters, our country and our people, the sphere of our family and the place of our dwelling, all of these were determined for us far ahead of time, and these all exert the most powerful influence on our entire existence and life. We ourselves derive from that community the basic shape of our physical and spiritual life, in terms of which no subsequent development can alter anything.

This significance of the family for the individual is increased still further by the fact that the unity of the family unfolds into the richest diversity. Every family has its own features; every family bears its own character, and all of its members have several features in common. There exists among them a community of kinship, but also a sharing of the life of the soul. How this happens we don't know, but there is a law whereby traits of parents are inherited by children and grandchildren, indeed, even from generation to generation and from century to century. The apple does not fall far from the tree, and a good child imitates his father. A community of kinship and of souls, of dispositions and interests, of various material and spiritual treasures, keeps members of a family together, despite occasionally being separated by distance, and distinguishes it together from all other homes and families. In every member of the family lives something of ourselves. The honor and the shame that others accord them we attribute to ourselves. In former times this sense of family was far stronger than it is today, and it was the source of all sorts of obligations. But it still continues to live on among us; it's in our blood; where it cannot walk upright, it crawls about. It betrays its strength even in its opposite, into which it occasionally changes. The wound inflicted upon the sense of family causes more pain than any other. There is no hatred more fierce than fraternal hatred. There are no sadder quarrels than those between family members; such quarrels harden into feuds. The proverb expresses bitterness that says: a person can choose his friends, but he is stuck with his family!

And still, this unity includes a remarkable diversity. The community of the family brings with it a treasury of relationships and qualities. The relation of husband and wife, of parents and children, of brothers and sisters, hardly exhausts this treasury, for the relationship that a husband enjoys with his wife is altogether different than the relationship a wife enjoys with her husband, and the relationship of parents with children differs from those between father and mother and the children together, and between each parent with each child, and in this way the same family life proceeds in ever greater specialization, as the number of members expands.

This is the case not only with the relationships but also with the qualities belonging to each family member. Masculine and feminine qualities, physical and spiritual strengths, intellectual, volitional, and emotional gifts, age and youth, strength and weakness, authority and obedience, affection and love, unity and diversity of interests, all of these come together in one family, unified and distinguished and blended together. The diversity both attracts and repels, unifies and isolates; sometimes the family is a small kingdom divided against itself, but such division can be intense because the unity is generally so deep and solid. From day to day that unity in diversity is maintained by the father, and especially by the mother; a communal language, religion, and morality, communal traditions, relationships, and interests, communal experiences of love and suffering, of joy and sorrow, of sickness and recovery, of death and grief, all preserve the unity and keep it in balance with the diversity.

The Family's Nurturing Power for Parents

All of these priceless qualities constitute the home as the first and best school of nurture that exists on earth. True enough, there are miserable families where one can speak only of a nurture unto sin and iniquity. Surely we should be grateful for the civil authority whereby in some cases the children are removed from such parental influence and entrusted to public institutions for their nurture; such is indeed terrible, but sometimes necessary, when the children need to be protected against their own parents, their natural protectors. We must, however, hope and labor for the situation where these cases remain the exception. For no other institution, whether through the efforts of particular individuals or societies, established through the church or through the state, can replace or compensate for the family.

Nowhere are that unity and community, that diversity and exchange, that forming element and that nurturing power encountered so richly as in the sphere of the family. In this respect, no art can improve upon nature, no science can improve upon life. So when some would point to miserable family conditions as an argument for gradually removing the nurture of the children from the parents and handing it over to the state, at that point let all the defenders and friends of the family join hands and cooperate unitedly to maintain and reform family life, which forms the healthy, natural foundation of society and church and state. And let a vigorous protest be sounded against all those who through immoral entertainment, low art, cheap novels, and sensuous performances violate the honor of marriage and undermine the foundations of the family!

We must realize that removing children from their parents would inflict an incalculable injury not only on the children, but also on the parents. Far and away most men and women are not at all fully prepared for nurturing when they enter into marriage, but they obtain the richest experience only once they have become married. Many a husband is a picture of clumsiness at the birth of his first child, and what do many wives know about care and nurture when they clasp their firstborn to their heart? But both learn in the school of life; and the experience of the family nurtures them further along as well—better than any educational institution could. Cooking school and family classes can render excellent assistance when past upbringing has been lacking. But the best homemakers and the best mothers come from families and are formed by the family itself. The family is a school for the children, but in the first place it is a school for the parents.

In our contemporary world, the husband is still the head of the family, even though his authority has in many respects been modified. Fortunately, it no longer consists in an absolute power over wife and children, nor is it any longer based on physical strength. It also does not rest in the fact that he is the family priest, the liturgist, the one performing religious ceremonies, and even less does it consist in the fact that he alone is the teacher and master of his children. For the state, the church, society, and the school have come to circumscribe and limit the rights and duties of the family from every side. Nor is the family nowadays any longer an industrial commune that alone provides entirely for its own subsistence. Even with respect to property the husband no longer enjoys such sovereign right as in earlier times; he cannot do with it as he pleases; in any case, life and customs and civil legislation are all moving in the direction of limiting the power of the husband in this respect.

Nevertheless, the husband is still the head of the family and is clothed with authority, not by virtue of the approval of his wife and his children, but on his own account, by virtue of the right bestowed by God. From the husband proceeds the choice of marriage partner, the power of procreation, the establishment and maintenance of the family. He is still priest, insofar as he leads in prayer and in reading God's Word, and attends to the religious interests of his household. He is still instructor and teacher, insofar as he provides leadership to his wife and children by means of greater wisdom, wider experience, and clearer judgment. He is still the head of his wife, insofar as he dwells with her not as a king over his subjects or a master over his slaves, but with understanding, honoring her as the weaker vessel, and as the stronger and bigger person he serves one who is weaker and smaller, loving and

Family and Nurture

protecting her, even as Christ does for his church. He is still the father of his children, not only by virtue of begetting them, but also insofar as he goes before them and leads them, encourages and strengthens them, warns and disciplines them. He is still the representative of the family outside the home, insofar as he gives the family his name, his position, his honor, functioning by acting in its name and serving its interests. People can differ about whether he may be considered worthy of exercising the privilege of participation through political vote merely and simply as family leader; but when he does so, he exercises that privilege not as an individual, but as the head of the family. In a word, the authority of the husband and father has in our society been significantly modified; it has received a far more rational, moral, and personal character, but it nonetheless continues in this modified form; in its essence it is indestructible.

The wife has a different place and task in the family. If the husband is the head, then the wife is the heart of the family. The husband brings in the fruits of his labor, the wife distributes them according to each one's need; the husband gives, the wife receives; the husband establishes the family, the wife preserves the family; the husband conceives the child, but the life of the child is intimately developed along with that of the mother far more than with that of the father; the husband lives in society, the wife lives in her family; the husband exercises "power directed outward and influence directed inward," the wife exercises "power directed inward and influence directed outward." Just as the husband is independent in his work and must nevertheless labor with a view to the interests of his family, so too the wife is independent within the family, but in such a way that she thereby remains bound to her husband through moral relationships. When according to his duty the husband brings in the reward of his toil for maintaining the family, then the wife takes that reward in receipt and apportions it according to the need of each. She organizes the household, arranges and decorates the home, and supplies the tone and texture of home life; with unequaled talent she magically transforms a cold room into a cozy place, transforms modest income into sizable capital, and despite all kinds of statistical predictions, she uses limited means to generate great things.

Within the family she preserves order and peace, because she knows the character of each person and knows how to supply the needs of each. She protects the weak, tends the sick, comforts the sorrowing, sobers the proud, and restrains the strong. Far more than the husband, she lives along with all her children, and for the children she is the source of comfort amid suffering, the source of counsel amid need, the refuge and fortress by day and by night. The heart of her husband trusts in her, and her children call her blessed [Prov. 31:10–28]. Both husband and wife nurture each other and are themselves formed by their children who were born from them. A marriage that remains childless is not thereby rendered purposeless, just as the life of an unmarried person need not be profitless. For husband and wife marriage is meaningful and is for them a means for fulfilling their earthly and spiritual calling. But just as marriage is to be recommended in general, so too a marriage blessed with children is what may generally be described as a customary, normal marriage. By father, mother, and child the family is built according to the aesthetic principle of beautiful symmetry.

Holy Scripture evaluates having children entirely differently than the modern generation. It teaches that a marriage blessed by God serves the extension of the human race and the subjection and dominion of the earth, and Scripture therefore views children as a blessing from God and as an inheritance of the Lord. For the wife the way to heavenly salvation lies paved in the family; in bringing forth and nurturing children she demonstrates the genuineness and the power of her Christian faith (1 Tim. 2:15), and for the husband the apostle's saying possesses a similar significance.

For children are the glory of marriage, the treasure of parents, the wealth of family life. They develop within their parents an entire cluster of virtues, such as paternal love and maternal affection, devotion and self-denial, care for the future, involvement in society, the art of nurturing. With their parents, children place restraints upon ambition, reconcile the contrasts, soften the differences, bring their souls ever closer together, provide them with a common interest that lies outside of them, and opens their eyes and hearts to their surroundings and for their posterity. As with living mirrors they show their parents their own virtues and faults, force them to reform themselves, mitigating their criticisms, and teaching them how hard it is to govern a person. The family exerts a reforming power upon the parents. Who would recognize in the sensible, dutiful father the carefree youth of yesterday, and who would ever have imagined that the lighthearted girl would later be changed by her child into a mother who renders the greatest sacrifices with joyful acquiescence? The family transforms ambition into service, miserliness into munificence, the weak into strong, cowards into heroes, coarse fathers into mild lambs, tenderhearted mothers into ferocious lionesses. Imagine there were no marriage and family, and humanity would, to use Calvin's crass expression, turn into a pigsty.

The Family's Nurturing Power for Children, Misunderstood by Recent Theories of Nurturing

Even stronger is the influence of the family on the children. Children are a blessing and an enrichment, but they place upon parents serious obligations and they are the object of their apprehensive concern for many years. In a certain sense one could say that a child's future depends upon that child's nurture. For that reason one may rejoice that in this century of research on the child, such comprehensive attention is being devoted to the child. The place that the child occupies today in the thinking, living, and conduct of civilized humanity is far greater than in previous centuries. In all countries and among all peoples, not only teachers and clergymen, but also health care and psychiatric professionals, jurists and sociologists are occupied with the study of the child. Organizations and associations, assemblies and congresses, church and state, are attracted to the interests of children. Family and school are no longer competent to fulfill the needs of children, but people are pushing additionally for various other institutions and forms of social assistance: safe houses, playgrounds, vacation resorts, pools, meals, clothes, reformatories, specialized institutions, children's courts, etc. Individuals, corporations, and government institutions assume care for abandoned, illegitimate, handicapped, neglected, and abused children. People long for the state to take charge, through legislation, of the protection and care of various kinds of impoverished children. From every side people are working with commendable effort for the future of the child.

Nevertheless, in the interests of the nurture that occurs in the family, it is not without benefit that in connection with this social activism for improving the lot of the child, we not lose sight of several things. First among them is that this activism is being guided consciously or unconsciously by the intention of having the nurture of children occur more and more *systematically*. People are moving toward the position that scientific technique must take the work out of the hands of nature. True enough, people have freed themselves from the onesidedness of intellectualism in that connection, at least to a certain degree. The days are past when people thought that intellectual development by itself would result in moral improvement. In this respect the ideas of teachers and childcare providers have undergone a remarkable change, and today they focus on the development of physical and motor skills, feeling and imagination, sense of beauty and strength of will. Intellectualistic nurture has made room in broad circles for the hygienic, the aesthetic, and the moral; here and there one even hears a call going up that presses for more appreciation of the religious element in nurture. Nevertheless, despite all of this, there is no trace of any change in principle and direction. Before and afterward the effort continues to be made to bring the entire physical and spiritual nurture of the child under the direction of technical experts. More than they did previously, people talk about practice but attempt nonetheless to focus that practice just as strongly toward theory.

The theory of nurture is further dominated by modern science. It has, so to speak, turned its back on abstract thought and academic contemplation and has turned its face toward reality. Clear and neutral observation of the facts must provide the foundation on which the structure of science is erected. But it is easily forgotten in that connection that one can never observe all those facts other than with one's own eyes, can never arrange and classify them other than by means of one's own understanding, and that therefore all observation and reflection always appears to be dominated by one or another theory. This comes to expression especially with the study of the human being. Generally the idea dominates today that the human being has gradually evolved from the animal, and that in the first years of life each human being traverses the series of stages of previous animal-like development. The human person has already traveled quite far along the path of development, and can still travel much further. For development is always ongoing; the human being is not yet finished, but is always in the making; actually the human being *is* not, but always *becomes*.

If one studies the human being in his or her becoming, if one investigates as accurately as possible how human beings gradually evolved from the animal in the past, and how each human being in particular replicates this development of the race in his or her own existence, then according to the idea held by many, one can thereby get to know the laws guiding that development and one can also then indicate the direction in which nurture must be steered. Nurture must be built upon psychology, on the accurate knowledge of the origin of the human soul; psychology in turn must rest upon biology, on the science of the origin and development of life; and biology is again dependent on human anthropology, according to which human development is a subsection and an offshoot of the eons-long process of living cells and organisms. Until now that development has occurred unconsciously; nature had its reins in hand. But now cultural man has evolved, with his consciousness and will, with his apprehension and aptitude; and he has the calling to relieve nature of its work and to labor with his scientific insight for the improvement of the human race. Artificial selection continues today, having replaced natural selection! Therefore we should let the pairing of spouses, the lifestyle of the pregnant woman, the physical and spiritual care of the child from his or her first day of life onward, come to stand under the oversight and control of science. Let the process of becoming human be placed under the direction of technical experts, for there lies the best hope for the future. The human being will gradually become ennobled, just like the flower and the plant, the horse and the cow; he *was* an animal, he *became* human, and under the discipline of science surely he will yet become an angel.

From this theory the conclusion naturally flows that the nurture belonging to the family is rendered suspect and in various ways distrusted. People point to the many unhappy families in which, due to the ignorance, reluctance, cruelty, and social poverty of the parents, the child is neglected, mistreated, and even reared for a life of crime and imprisonment. And they don't stop there, but go on to point out all kinds of faults and shortcomings in ordinary middle-class households; parents have no time, opportunity, or aptitude for nurturing their children, they never study the subject, they are not well-informed about hygiene, physiology, or psychology. Radical improvement will come only when the nurture of children soon after birth is entrusted to specialists and put into the hands of experts. In this way the expectation for the future of the human race comes to focus more and more on the state.

The family cannot satisfy the scientific demands for nurture; let these become more and more a concern of the government. This is what one hears as people defend with complete seriousness the proposition that the state is the *natural* caregiver for children, not only the children who are poor, impoverished, neglected, mistreated, and inadequately cared for, but also the children of the rich and affluent. Only then will the ideal be achieved, when all children belong to the state. And when the objection is raised that in large numbers and to a large extent parents will abuse such a calling given to the state and will transfer the entire burden to the government's shoulders, then people answer in good conscience that this is not so bad. For in the first place, the state will transfer all the costs that it incurs back to the citizens; and secondly, the state itself has a very great deal of interest in such a large number of children. The first duty of the state is to maintain the human race. Children are the most expensive possession of a nation, the greatest national treasure and the strongest national power; by caring for the children, the state sustains itself. In this way everything is being arranged more and more so that the natural household nurture provided by the family is being nudged out by the systematic and artificial nurture through or on behalf of the state.

The difference of opinion in this connection does not involve whether the state has any interest in the health and welfare, the education and nurture of its citizens. It is also obvious that in special cases where society cannot salvage things by itself, the government offers support, protects the weak, and comes to the rescue of the oppressed. In this way, for example, nobody would withhold his consent with and commendation for the laws protecting children. But everything depends on the question how one views and evaluates the intervention of the state with respect to nurture. Does this activity belong to the natural calling of the state, or is its assistance summoned and accepted only because existing needs either are not or cannot be met in any other way? Is the nurture that the government offers in its schools and institutions the entire nurture a child needs, or does it serve merely to supplement the nurture that is given to the child in the family? To whom does the task of nurturing belong in the first place, to the family or to the state, to the parents or to the experts, to practice or to theory, to life or to science?

A powerful, continually growing stream is moving in the direction of technically expert and artificial nurture. Just like the advocates of free love point with a certain relish to the many unhappy marriages in order to bring legal and lawful marriage into disrepute, so too defenders of government childcare seize with eagerness upon all the miseries and faults of home childcare to thereby strengthen their theory and to recommend it as the only real and adequate solution. They use examples of unhappy families not to press for reforming and improving family life, but on the contrary, to undermine the parental home as a nurturing institution and to build a new system of breeding and raising children on the ruins of the family.

The Imbalance of These Theories

In opposition to these advocates of state absolutism, however, many people fortunately are seeking to protect the family against the attacks to which it is currently exposed, by calling out to us loudly and vigorously: "Do not forget the family when it comes to nurture, and within the family, do not forget the mother especially!" For this warning, they have at hand nature and history, people's rational understanding and religious-moral principles.

Depreciating the nurture provided by the family is usually accompanied by an exaggerated estimate of the power of nurture. Under the influence of the supposition that at this point human beings have already traveled wonderfully far along the path of evolution, people surrender to the illusion that human beings can still do infinitely more, and that we can make human beings into whatever we want. If only full use were made of the results that have been and will be obtained by scientific investigation, then nurture would not only furnish outward formation and intellectual development, but it would also improve the human person morally, eliminating the brutish inclinations still at work internally, renewing his heart, and bringing sin and crime to an end, not all at once but gradually. When people apply this expectation regarding nurture as a yardstick for measuring that nurture which nowadays is being defended within the family under the guidance of Christian principles, people naturally arrive at a very unsatisfactory and disappointing conclusion. Family nurture has hardly lived up to that expectation, and although it has been active already for many centuries, Christianity has contributed precious little to the improvement of the human race. Sin has not diminished, crime has not decreased, and the prisons are as full as they have ever been. Such a notion, however, regarding the omnipotence of nurture conflicts irreconcilably with all the facts drawn from observation. It crashes headlong into the sober reality that every human being is born small and weak, helpless and needy, sinful and unclean, and that therefore all education and nurture must start anew at the beginning with every human being. Culture can surely contribute some improvement in terms of outward forms and social circumstances, and Christianity has also played a significant role in that; but human nature remains constant, its capacities and powers constantly hover near average, and from the human heart constantly proceed the same evil thoughts and imaginations. For centuries already children have been taught reading, writing, and arithmetic, but at present no one is born already possessing these skills, and everyone must learn them from the ground up. It would be just as silly to blame the [need for] education in these skills for the fact that the human race has not progressed even one step further; it would be just as senseless to make family nurture responsible for the fact that every child anew is conceived and born in sin. Nurture is not omnipotent; it possesses great significance and far-reaching influence, but it is limited by the human nature a person receives and cannot alter internally. To demand from nurture that it must perfect humanity places upon parents an unbearable burden, discourages them instead of supporting and fortifying them, and engenders nothing but bitter disappointment.

After all, the advocates of a technically expert program of nurture can talk rather easily. Without great difficulty they can assemble the numerous faults that cling to nurture in the home, and then promise the pot of gold at the end of the rainbow for those who buy the theory they are advocating but which they have never implemented and which will never be capable of implementation. This boils down to exactly the same thing we get with the portrait of the socialist welfare state. If someone criticizes this welfare state and shows that it cannot exist, then this criticism is rebutted with the evasive claim that socialism does not assign any value to such a portrait and leaves the organization of the welfare state to evolution. If someone objects that socialism does not know where it wants to lead us and thus may not coax us into embracing its theory, then once again without blinking an eye, their fantastic portrait of the future is presented and displayed to the masses in all its glowing colors. In the same way, many expect a powerful, moral advancement of humanity from a new approach to child-rearing. But when that expectation is investigated more carefully, people see that it is built on sand.

After all, the foundation of this new, systematic nurture is, as they say, put in place by science. Now of course we may not speak ill of such a benefactor as science. Not only has it increased our knowledge and expanded our dominion throughout the ages; but especially in recent times it has rendered inestimable service to practical living. In many respects the fruit of its labor has produced much good for nurture in family and school. Who would not gladly listen to the wise counsel that science provides concerning the lifestyle of the pregnant woman, about the care of both healthy and sick children, regarding the requirements for nutrition and clothing, about adequate sunlight and fresh air, about work and rest, the arrangement of desks and classrooms, about overtaxing the brain, overstimulating the nerves, exercising the muscles, and about hundreds of other things besides? But science can never replace living; it can fortify living, guide and improve living, but never take its place. Just as agriculture owes many improvements to science, but nevertheless remains dependent on nature, on soil and climate, on rain and sunshine, on sowing and harvesting, so child-rearing can be assisted and supported by science but can never be appropriated by science or assigned to science. Even less so because all those sciences relating to childcare are still deficient and repeatedly change their conclusions. For example, in psychology there are just as many opinions as there are practitioners of this science regarding the origin and nature, the capacities and power, the development and function of the life of the soul. Any child-rearing that wishes to derive its principle and method from science would be embarrassed by the choice it had to follow and would be shaken in its faith every day. Any nurture that wished to proceed in a strictly technically expert manner and wished to rest purely on a scientific foundation would naturally acquire a very artificial character. That applies to every elementary school as well. People can organize schools to be as friendly as ever, with an education that resembles real life as closely as ever, and with a teacher who is equipped with sufficient knowledge and who has a heart filled with love for the children; it's still just a school. The instruction is administered to a particular number of children, within a fixed number of hours, according to a prescribed curriculum, corresponding with a previously developed method. It cannot be any different; the essence of the school, the character of its instruction, the fruit of its labor are all involved here.

The Family As the Nurturing Institution Par Excellence

But this entire regulation would be still more artificial if the entire life of the child must follow the course set by science. Thereby the child himself with his individuality would be sacrificed to the system, and childcare would be reduced to training. Giving credit where credit is due, this training has its good side and is beneficial in its place. In contemporary society, with its many demands and multiplicity of examinations and tests, it is indispensable. One needs a certain discipline of the intellect and the will, of the memory and judgment, of physical exercise and motor development. But for that reason we value all the more the fact that the family is more important than the school, that practice is more important than theory, and life is more important than instruction.

The family is and remains the nurturing institution par excellence. Beyond every other institution it has this advantage, namely, that it was not constructed and artificially assembled by man. A man chooses a woman to be his wife, and a woman chooses a man to be her husband, but if things go well, they don't so much choose one another as they are chosen by each other; by means of a secret bond, in a manner ineffable, they are brought to each other. Children are then born from their intimate fellowship, but those children are granted to them, having a different sexuality, a different nature, a different disposition—perhaps different than what the parents would have wished and, had it been up to them, would have given their children. The family is no fabrication of human hands; it is a gift of God, bestowed according to his good pleasure. Even though the family has existed for centuries, we cannot create a likeness; it was, it is, and it will continue to be a gift, an institution that God alone sustains.

Furthermore, the family does not consist of a number of empty forms that we need to fill, but it is full of life. The husband and wife, coming from differing families, each contributes their own genetic makeup, tradition, nature, character, disposition, and life. And each child born to them is a member of humanity, a person with capacities like those of everyone else, and yet distinguished from all those others, whose relation is close or distant, with a unique existence and character. A wealth of relationships, a multiplicity of characteristics, a treasure trove of gifts, a world of love, a wonderful intermingling of rights and duties—all of these, once again, are brought together not by human determination but by God's sovereign determination. A novelist, a playwright or poet, can portray a number of types, but exhausts the choices available; the characters described in subsequent works are often copies of what has appeared already in his earlier work. But there is no end to the variety present in real people; for what is involved is an almighty, omniscient, creating power. For that, the family is the primary and preeminent revelation.

Therefore the nurture that takes place within the family possesses a very special character. Even as the family itself cannot be imitated, so too one cannot make a copy of family nurture. No school, no boarding school, no day-care center, no government institution can replace or improve upon the family. The children come from the family, grow up in the family, without themselves knowing how. They are formed and raised without themselves being able to account for that. The nurture provided by the family is entirely different than that provided by the school; it is not bound to a schedule of tasks and does not apportion its benefits in terms of minutes and hours. It consists not only in instruction, but also in advice and warning, leading and admonition, encouragement and comfort, solicitude and sharing. Everything in the home contributes to nurture—the hand of the father, the voice of the mother, the older brother, the younger sister, the infant in the bassinet, the sickly sibling, grandmother and grandchildren, uncles and aunts, guests and friends, prosperity and adversity, celebrations and mourning, Sundays and workdays, prayers and thanksgiving at mealtime and the reading of God's Word, morning devotions and evening devotions. Everything is serviceable for nurturing each other day by day, hour by hour, without plan, without appointment, without technique, all of which are set beforehand. Everything possesses power to nurture, apart from being able to analyze and calculate that power. Thousands of incidents, thousands of trivia, thousands of trifles all exert their influence. It is life itself that nurtures, that cultivates the rich, inexhaustible, multifaceted, magnificent life. The family is the school of life, because it is the fountain and hearth of life.

Such nurture encompasses the whole person. In school, life is cut up into segments; in school, we find the nurture of the intellect, of the memory, of the will, of the character, of emotions, of imagination, and still other forms of nurture. Alternately, to the degree that a segment is either favored or neglected, one is forced either to abandon or restrict, on the one hand, or to supplement or expand a particular subject of instruction. But a family does not operate with such apportioned attention. Everything is integrated and unified, like the blossom within the bud. The child does indeed learn within the family and receives instruction; the child gradually becomes oriented within his surroundings and gets to know his small world, expressing a multitude of observations, emotions, imaginations, words, and thoughts; in terms of proportion, the child learns more in his early years than in subsequent years. But all of this happens unnoticed, automatically, gradually, uninterruptedly; it is life that nurtures and it does so through life and for life. The powers of observation, memory, and judgment are exercised, but also the powers of imagination, of the will, of conscience, of character, and of the heart, as are the muscles and the nerves, together with the head, hands, and feet. Vices are resisted—stubbornness, selfishness, and jealousy; virtues are cultivated—purity, order, obedience, cooperation, compassion—as in no other school. A person's becoming human occurs within the home; here the foundation is laid for the forming of the future man and woman, of the future father and mother, of the future member of society, of the future citizen, of the future subject in the kingdom of God.

9

FAMILY AND SOCIETY

The Concept of Society

The history of the human race did not begin atomistically, with a group of isolated individuals, but organically, with a marriage and a family. From the very beginning all those relationships were embedded in seed form within that family, relationships which would later arise among people in the most splendid manner. The disparity, which we presently observe everywhere in human society, is in principle and in essence not a result of sin, as many people thought in earlier and later times, but it existed from the very beginning, even before sin entered the world. Such disparity was willed by God for all his creatures and rests upon his good pleasure.

Within the first family, the distinctions between man and woman, parents and children, brothers and sisters, were already present, and along with them was supplied in seed form all those relationships of authority and obedience, coordination and subordination, parity and fraternity, which now in various expressions and concrete ways still govern the social life of human beings. Even as one star differs in brightness from another star; even as all physical bodies are not the same, but can be distinguished as a human body or an animal or a fish or a bird; even as in the state of glory there will be a diversity of gifts and strengths and various degrees of blessedness;[1] so too the human race has unfolded on earth according to God's will, in an endless diversity of persons and powers, relationships and capacities, talents and gifts, possessions and goods. From that first family have come clans and tribes and nations, and among those nations a rich group association has developed, which we generally refer to as society.

The word *society* is related to the French *societe*, and the Latin *societas*, which itself is based on *socius*, which means "companion." Hence, the word *society* has come to refer to a group of people living together in an ordered community. A society is formed when individuals who agree, sympathize, and cooperate with each other pursue general or special interests, and therefore enjoy trustful concourse with one another. In recent times people often speak about a society among insects and animals—among bees, for example, or among ants and beetles. In the animal world we discover genuine social and cooperative features that surprise us and display remarkable traces of similarity with human society. But just as animals and people are similar at many points, but are nonetheless members of different species, so too the analogy existing between their respective forms of group behavior does not prove any identity of behavior. Whatever similarities exist, there are also significant essential differences between them. The psycho-spiritual traits of language, religion, morality, etc., which constitute the preeminent elements

---

[1] Ed. note: Bavinck believed that a diversity of gifts, talents, and rewards for faithful obedience would exist in the state of glorification, and he developed this understanding in the concluding chapter of the final volume of his *Reformed Dogmatics*. He is not teaching that some believers enjoy higher degrees of salvation than others. For an English translation, see "The Renewal of Creation" (chap. 18) in Herman Bavinck, *Reformed Dogmatics: Holy Spirit, Church, and New Creation*, vol. 4, ed. John Bolt, trans. John Vriend (Grand Rapids: Baker Academic, 2008), 715–30.

of human society, are totally absent in the animal world; there is no manufacturing of implements among animals; they neither know nor make anything of history. So when we discuss the notion of *society*, we may properly take human society as our starting point.

Now a society can arise among people, and frequently does, by means of agreement and contract, and varies from a club, an association, or a company. It is established intentionally for the shared maintenance of a number of interests, some material, some spiritual, and it rests exclusively on voluntary human decision. Thus, we can speak of a farming and livestock association, of trade and industry groups, but also of literary clubs and charity organizations, of the arts and sciences, indeed, even of a society on behalf of the citizenry.

The word *society* points not only to the kind of coalition of people that arises through voluntary association and is established for an agreed-upon purpose. The same word is used frequently to refer to the kind of group of people that arises naturally in terms of various life relationships in mutual fellowship, something that is neither artificial nor juridical, but an organic, social entity. This kind of organic society can be understood in a broader and in a narrower sense. We might think of a group of people who live in a particular country and within a certain nation, and then we speak, for example, of the Greek society, or the Roman society, the French or the English society. We might expand the concept still further to include the organized association of people living on a continent, affected by certain historical influences, or spread across the entire globe, and thus we speak of Western society or Eastern civilization or Christian culture or Muslim culture, of European or American society—referring then to various societies in general.

A person becomes a member of society understood in its organic, social meaning, not by voluntary agreement, but by nature through birth and life. No person is merely an individual; a single individual is not a person. Above the entrance to the history of humanity stands written this saying: "It is not good that the man should be alone" [Gen. 2:18]. From conception onward, a human being is a product of fellowship; every person is born from, and in, fellowship; persons are cared for and nurtured in the context of fellowship, and continue in some kind of fellowship throughout life, all the way to one's final breath. A human being is a convivial creature and remains so, all the hermits and bachelors notwithstanding.

But this organic society can develop in different directions, and be manifested in various forms. When it consists of the union of husband and wife and the children born to them, it is termed a *family*; despite the inescapable difference of scale, every family is a society in miniature. When it appears in the political arena and identifies its purpose as maintaining, protecting, and fortifying a nation, it is termed a *state*. When it is involved in the preaching and applying of God's Word, it functions as a *church*. But distinct from all these forms of association is that human concourse which comes to expression in language and mores, in law and custom, in science and art, in career and business, in castes and classes, and which ordinarily is identified in the narrower sense of the word nowadays with the term *society*. As such, society is distinguished from family, church, and state, it has its own existence and life, and it spans an entire, broad range of human thought and action.

The Boundaries of Society with Respect to Family, Church, and State

Very different sentiments exist with regard to circumscribing this society. Some would exclude the family, since the family forms the foundation of society and is not simply one element of society; others view society simply as the development and expanding of family life. According to the one opinion, society is so essentially distinct from the state that it has no need whatsoever of the state for its existence and development. According to the other view, society is a product of the state, called into existence through the state's judicial constitution and legislation, and dependent on the state for its continuation. There are those who see religion and the church as nothing more than a fruit of human culture; while others would maintain the independence of religion and the church, seeing them as belonging to the foundation of society rather than to the components of society. Finally, whereas some restrict society to the acquisition and distribution of material goods, others expand society to include production and distribution of spiritual goods as well; economists usually understand society to refer only to the aggregate of household relationships and components among a nation, whereas sociologists usually understand society as broadly as possible, seeking to annex all human relationships and phenomena. All these important scientific questions need not be discussed here, much less resolved; we may suffice here with a twofold comment.

The first is this, that out of regard for its own interests every science must restrict itself to that which comprises its domain. Economics is thus fully within its right to investigate only the household relationships and efforts of human society. To the same degree sociology loses its scientific character when it seeks to draw everything within its purview, when it pronounces about everything, and when it loses its focus through philosophical generalities. In the second place, one should keep in mind that society is not limited to acquiring and distributing material goods, even though people make this a unique object of investigation. Because a person consists of body and soul, and simultaneously comprises a spiritual and a sensory being, society also always possesses a number of ideal, spiritual goods that are closely related to material culture, but that nevertheless have an independent value. Subduing the earth in the broadest sense is the content and goal of culture, but this subduing is possible only through human knowledge and ability; and these proceed in the proper direction only when they are guided by religious and moral principles; dominion over the earth is an unfolding of the image of God in humanity. Therefore society must be understood in the broader sense of the word as referring to the entire form of human association willed by God, grounded in nature, and coming to gradual development in history, which comes to manifestation in the combination and cooperation of the gifts and powers granted to humanity, and which has as its goal the preservation and generation, the distribution and enjoyment, of various spiritual and material goods.

Formulated in this sense, one could reasonably claim that society is a discovery of a more recent time. Only gradually has the perspective developed in which the social life of humanity was not restricted to family, state, and church. Alongside and among these institutions an immeasurably rich arena of human living and human effort has come to be introduced during the course of history, which has come to require increasing attention. Whereas in former times history writing focused principally on royalty and nobility, together with national political events and wars, nowadays people prefer to focus on the populace, on the social circumstances and the elements of culture. It is not surprising that this interest in culture has awakened relatively late; in terms of the wealth of living that confronts us, society itself is the product of a long history and has achieved its independent position only gradually.

True enough, society was in principle already embedded organically in the family, from which the human race had its origin. That fact, however, does not constitute the family as equivalent to society; even as the acorn contains the oak in seed form, whose growth requires various factors (soil, climate, etc.), so too society emerged from the family only gradually and under the influence of various circumstances. Something else of significance must be mentioned. The development of the human race has not been normal. Had sin not entered the world, human society would probably have developed patriarchally and would have expanded as one large association of families. If, however, after the entrance of sin, the human race was to survive, the institution of the church and the state was necessary.

The church was instituted in principle when the promise was given concerning the seed of the woman, he who would contend against the seed of the serpent and destroy his head. This church lived on in the families of the patriarchs, assumed a national form among Israel, and on Pentecost came to exist independently of both state and society. Likewise, the state was instituted in principle with the right that God bestowed upon mankind after the flood, together with the duty that God assigned to mankind to punish the murderer with death. Murder was forbidden because, in distinction from the animal, a man was created in God's image and even in his sinful state continued to display remnants thereof. God did not keep for himself the execution of punishment against the murderer, but he transferred it to mankind. Thereby man himself was clothed with authority and power over other people who had violated the image of God; from now on the state existed in principle as the institution that bears the sword of justice.

Family, state, and church each share this feature, that each is independent of the other, each has its own origin and purpose, and none came forth from the other. They differ, however, in the fact that the family is the oldest institution and came into existence immediately with the creation of the first human couple; the state and the church, however, were instituted after the fall, and in such a way that the church owes its existence to special grace, while the state owes its existence to common grace. Society corresponds most closely to the family; even apart from sin, society would have developed from the family, and the relationships within which society is manifested are expansions and indications of the fundamental forms found in the family. Authority and obedience, independence and subordination, equality and inequality, correspondence and variation, unity of nature and diversity of gifts and callings—all these have been present in the family from the very beginning, and in no sense came into existence as a result of sin.

Even so, one cannot claim that society is nothing else than and no more than a smaller or larger group of families that live alongside each other. For a society exists for the first time when among different people there develop not merely family relationships but also economic (household) relationships, when the various gifts and powers bestowed upon people connect them together and bring their products into circulation. Such an association, cooperation, and exchange, came into existence very gradually, however. For the oldest form in which people lived together was the patriarchal family; such a family consisted not only of parents and children, but also of grandparents and grandchildren and anyone else belonging to a family, and then additionally also the servants and maids. It possessed a very large degree of independence, for the patriarchal family brought everything forth that it needed for its survival and continuation. With its own means and through its own powers it acquired food and drink, blankets and clothing, dwelling and furnishings, weapons and tools. There were not yet any independent careers and professions, no carpenters and bricklayers, no bakers and clothiers; each family had to care for itself and was thereby in large measure independent of others.

Changes in Society Resulting from the Need for Camaraderie and from Work

Especially two causes occasioned gradual change here. First, the need for camaraderie, unique to men, drove them out of their homes in order to unite with others for various purposes. The wife by nature is attached to the home; intergenerational life occupies a much more important place for her; in terms of housekeeping and childcare she discovers a task that monopolizes her life; in this way the home is her world and the family is the focal point of her labor. But with the husband life is arranged entirely differently; he makes friends entirely differently than the wife; he never finds full satisfaction at home but goes out looking for other things that attract his interest. He seeks fellowship with others who are close to him in age and disposition; and together they form a club or an association in order to join at set times in play or amusement, hunting or fishing, pursuing political or social interests.

Alongside family bonds, other voluntary connections gradually arise between men of a similar sort. Family relationships are established through kinship and they exist by nature, and the wife is their most powerful protector, with whom the sense of family is far more strongly developed than with the husband. But clubs do not exist by nature, being formed rather by choice, and as a rule they arise not among women but among men.[2] Such groups or associations of men appear among all peoples and have had influential significance for social relationships. Not infrequently opposition and conflict arise between families and convivial associations. The man who is always home, who has no social or political interests and is not a member of any outside group, easily becomes a "domestic" or a "busybody in the kitchen"; and the man who returns to his friends a few weeks after his wedding and regularly attends club and group meetings runs the serious risk later of entirely neglecting his wife and children. But no matter how severely both kinds of organizational relationships can come into conflict with each other, they are both indispensable, they rest upon the different nature of man and woman, and each contributes to the enrichment of life and to the development of the community.

Another cause responsible for the development of society is found in work. The first human beings received the mandate to cultivate and care for the garden in which they lived, to fill the earth, to subdue and rule over it. Dominion is inseparable from the image of God according to which people were created. Sin did indeed introduce an immense change in the image of God, but insofar as human beings still display the image of God, they also retain the calling and the power to subdue the earth. Therefore the poet of Psalm 8 could sing of the glory of God radiating throughout the whole world, especially in terms of puny human beings having been made a little lower than the angels, crowned with honor and glory, beholding all the works of God's hands in subjection to them. Work, then, is certainly made more difficult and onerous as

---

2 Ed. note: There is a rich contemporary literature on the sociological dimensions of associational life that would challenge Bavinck's viewpoint here. There are also important differences in the fundamental structure of associational life in Europe and North America. For more on this, see Alexis de Tocqueville's *Democracy in America* (1835–40).

a result of sin—many languages use the same word for "work" and "difficulty" or "trouble"—but work existed before the fall; it was included in being created in God's image and consisted in subjecting the earth in terms of what nowadays is referred to as culture. In its widest sense, culture is nothing else than subjugating the earth, saturating the material with the spirit, wielding and applying human knowledge and ability with respect to the world around us.

People misconstrue this character of work when they do not continually keep in view the relationship between work and being created in the image of God. Work is rooted in human beings as rational beings and is a likeness of the work that God accomplishes through creation and providence. Presently this is construed altogether differently, when people entertain the notion that human beings developed gradually from the animals, that people are driven by need and misery toward ever nobler exertion. In this view, every component of civilization and culture, not only knowledge and art but also religion and morality, intellect and will, reason and conscience, are the fruit of labor and are acquired in the struggle to live. Such a view does contain this truth, namely, that struggle and need often compel human beings to exert all of their powers; nothing teaches us to pray like being in need, as the proverb says; so one could also say that being in need makes one resourceful, and that the hero is born amid struggle. Still, one must not forget that although struggle and need do stimulate people to use those gifts that they possess but that often unconsciously lie dormant, nevertheless they cannot create what does not exist, and people cannot invent new gifts and powers. Work does not *make* a person a rational, moral, and religious being, but presupposes that one *is* such a being; in work, a person's humanity comes to light.

Therefore all work displays a spiritual and a material side. The human being consists of soul and body both in one person, and shows this in all his work. Certainly it is the case that in one kind of work the spiritual side comes to the fore, while in another kind of work the physical side predominates. But even in the most spiritual work, a person exerts the body more or less, the philosopher thinks, but only with his brains; the day laborer works with his hands, but also needs his soul, his mental acumen. For that reason, it is regrettable that the word *work* has obtained such a one-sided meaning, and usually refers only to working with one's hands. Scripture puts it differently, speaking, in connection with the servant of the Lord, of the labor of his soul (Isa. 53:11), talking of working in wisdom, knowledge, and skill (Eccles. 2:21), and often identifying the activity of the apostles with the term *work*. There is no single distinct class of workers, but all people are workers, created in God's image, ordained for his service. All work bears and ought to bear a human, that is, a rational and a moral character.

This explains why religion and civilization, cultus and culture, Christianity and humanness exist together in such an intimate relationship. All progress in civilization and culture is dependent on the religious-moral life of humanity. All of history serves as proof of this. When religion and morality deteriorate among a nation, they drag down with them the best and most refined culture. Intellectual development, material prosperity, wealth, and luxury are in themselves excellent things; but when they are severed from the root of religion, they serve to advance evil far more than they arrest and restrain it. No enduring civilization exists without a healthy religious and moral life. Those who forsake God need to fear pain upon pain, but those who trust in him, in him alone, will be surrounded by his kindnesses.

The Power of Labor and Material of Labor

Seen from the viewpoint of labor, one can say that the human being is the integrating center of all kinds of powers associated with labor. These powers associated with work are hardly equal among all people; in this respect as well, there are poor and rich, not in the first place as a result of sin, but of nature. There is a difference of work-strength between man and woman, parents and children; there is distinction among gifts of the soul and capacities of the body; one receives four, another five, a third only one talent. But each person has received a gift; and in general, a person is the sum total of manpower; he can work with his soul and with his body, with his observation and perception, memory and imagination, intellect and reason, head and hand, arm and foot, shoulders and back. Specifically in this connection, the soul functions primarily through the *intellect* while the body functions primarily through the *hand*. These are very special powers associated with work; through the intellect, a human being elevates himself above the animal, he knows and "understands," he apprehends in his consciousness things outside of himself, making them his own spiritual property, and acquires dominion, knowledge, and power. Through the hand he similarly elevates himself above the animal, grasps something, holds on to it, lifts it and lowers it, realizes his ideas and wishes in the world outside himself, turns it into a work of his spirit and stamps it with his personality; with the hand, one "handles" and is "handy"; the hand is the organ of human dominion.

But with the intellect and the hand, a person is in a position to expand and strengthen the powers of work residing in his spiritual-sensory nature. Through the intellect he acquires knowledge, insight, and wisdom; through the hand he employs tools; through the intellect he enlists science in service to his labor, through the hand he enlists technological tools in service to his labor, and in the widest sense: art is born. Man is a thinking being and skilled in using tools, the one not separated from the other, but both joined together. Science and technology are related, going back to the earliest origins of the human race, and they develop in fellowship with one another.

The notion is incorrect that our current age would be the first era of science and technology. Of course we are seeing a remarkable advance in both, but this became possible only on the basis of previous centuries. As the child learns the basic ideas and concepts in the earliest years, with which he then later works, so too in the beginning of the human race there was an extraordinarily rich development. Humanity was not sent into the world naked and empty-handed, but from the beginning functioned with a reservoir of competencies and aptitudes; throughout history there have always been periods of renaissance in knowledge and art, science and technology. When we study the earliest history of humanity, we encounter in Babylon and Egypt, in China and India, not a wild horde of people but highly civilized nations with a wealth of science and an immense technological aptitude. The extraordinary glorification of our present century rests in large part on ignorance about earlier times.

By means of science and technology, a person expands his own capacity for work. Science expands the human spirit, technology expands the human body. Someone has correctly observed that all our tools are extensions and refinements of our physical organs. Especially the hand, this human tool par excellence, has served as an example of this. The hammer simulates the forearm, the cup simulates the hollow of the hand, the pencil extends the finger. Our decimal system derives from our ten fingers, and the foot represents our unit of measurement. Our eye serves as the model for spectacles and binoculars, our ear for the telephone. The musical instrument known as the organ corresponds to our lungs, the pump resembles our heart. Our nerves are the "cables running through our body," and telegraph cables are the "nerves of humanity." In a word, a person invents tools with his own soul, his own thought, his own life; in technology man copies himself, but at the same time elevates, energizes, and extends his work capacity; even the rhythm of his work displays the poetry of his own soul.

But work capacity and tools are not enough to achieve something. Human beings cannot create anything, cannot make something appear out of nothing, like God can. Man is bound to the earth, is earthly, from the earth, and thus needs an object on which to exercise his capacity for work and thereby form something new. People need the earth itself not only when they begin their work but even beforehand for maintaining their capacity for work and for producing their tools. The capacity for work that people possess in soul and body is not an immutable entity, but must repeatedly be replenished and increased; just like the fireplace cannot heat without being replenished with wood, so too a person cannot live if he doesn't eat. And people need the world, with its plant kingdom and animal kingdom, its soil and climate, day and night, light and darkness, rain and sunshine, for food and drink, covering and clothing, for protection against cold and heat, for their activity and their rest. Similarly people need nature in order to produce their tools; and human ingenuity is surprising when it comes to making natural forces serviceable to their desires; the mineral kingdom yields coal, peat, and metals; the plant kingdom supplies them with vegetables and various kinds of wood; the animal kingdom offers them sheep and cattle, the animals of the field, the birds of the sky, and the fish of the sea. People place all of them in service and with them they fortify their own powers. Sunlight and fresh air, wind and weather, steam and electricity are tools in their hands for work. They conquer all of nature, which is inexhaustible in its power; every second the sun sends thirty-six billion horsepower of light to this earth,[3] of which half evaporates into the atmosphere and the other half is used by the earth and its inhabitants.

But as we said, people need the earth not only for maintaining and fortifying their capacity for work; it is just as necessary for the exercise of that capacity. A person must have an object to which they may transfer their work capacity, material to be worked, substance to be manipulated. A person cannot live in a vacuum. In his intellectual, moral, and religious life, he is tied to the world; he must have something about which to think, or else he loses himself in idle speculations; there must be light and color if he is to

---

[3] Ed. note: Bavinck employs the antiquated unit of measurement "horsepower of light" (*paard* means "*horse*" and *kracht* means "*power*") to indicate the scope of the sun's immense amount of energy output to earth. The standard contemporary measurement used to calculate solar radiation or insolation is the Langley Unit. The langley (Ly) is a unit of energy distribution over area. One langley is one thermochemical calorie per square centimeter. In SI units, one langley is 41840.00 J/m^2 (or joules per square meter). The unit was named after Samuel Pierpont Langley (1834–1906) in 1947.

see anything, there must be sounds if he is to hear anything; there must be divine revelation if his religious and moral life are to possess genuine content. And in the same way a person needs material things to do his physical work, in order to use his strength; to bake bread he needs grain; to build a house he needs wood and iron, stone and glass. Human beings can never create anything, but only recreate and reshape. But in so doing, they show once again the extraordinary ingenuity of the human spirit. For under his hands, all of nature is an object of his work capacity. He uses even the seemingly useless and worthless for his purpose; he uses waste products to fertilize the land, and recycles newsprint into writing paper.

Complaints against Society and against Its Inequality

Through all this work that people perform in the world, there arises an immeasurable wealth of goods that vary widely in quality and value, but together constitute the treasure and capital of the human race. These include goods that display a more ideal character, like science and art; there are others of a more material nature, that function in terms of people's living necessities, like food and clothing, house and furniture. Some goods serve in terms of immediate consumption and enjoyment, like food and drink; others extend their usefulness by serving in the production of new goods, like machines and factories; the same object can serve for immediate consumption and again for extending the usefulness of other things, like a stove can serve for warming and for cooking.

For that reason one can expand the notion of goods to include the means and tools of labor that are used for producing other goods and that represent a significant asset; thus one can include among such goods fresh air, sunlight, wind, and water, although they were not produced through human labor, but are accessible to everybody; and the powers of labor bestowed upon a person in soul and body are in turn goods, rich and complete gifts, coming down from the Father of lights [James 1:17]. Even the many-faceted and infinitely varied relationships among people that arise as a result of labor, through agriculture, animal husbandry, business, manufacturing, science, art, etc., are goods whose value cannot be calculated in monetary terms. To put it simply, along with and built upon the foundation of the family, society itself, as a grand totality and inestimable good, is a priceless gift from the Creator and Sustainer of all things.

Currently, however, society is only seldom understood in this way. On the contrary, it is under attack from all sides and viewed as the cause of every misery and malady. Nowadays people shift all the blame from themselves and assign it to the terrible organization of society. Improve society, so they say, and you will automatically make people happy and good! Now of course there are numerous abuses in society that nobody wants to defend. But one must not forget that those abuses have hardly existed only in our current society alone but in all times and places and often much worse than now. Everyone agrees that social circumstances have improved in many respects and deserve to be much preferred over those encountered in previous centuries and among non-Christian nations. Moreover, abuses exist not only in society, but also in the state, in the church, in the family, wherever people live; one finds them even in inanimate nature, which experiences the worst disasters through downpours and thunderstorms. There is nowhere in the whole world where one can flee to escape these miseries; and if one avoids them in one's own surroundings, one still always hosts them within one's own heart and will encounter them there. That there are abuses in society is not surprising; it would be astonishing if it were otherwise.

When one investigates carefully, it will become apparent that the intense struggle against society actually does not focus, at least not exclusively, on the abuses arising in society, but against the foundations on which society rests. Those abuses provide the occasion, but not the deepest cause, of the struggle. Even if those abuses could be eliminated through individual initiative or through the legislation of the state, these would not lead to the return of contentment and peace.

Universal suffrage, government pensions, insurance laws, social legislation, model factories, and whatever else one may cite, none of them would eliminate the resistance being mounted against society itself in terms of its present foundations. The deepest complaint against which conflict is being targeted is *inequality*, which exists everywhere. Political revolution, so people say, has made people equal before the state; if that is not to remain an incomplete effort, it must be finished in terms of social revolution, which will make people socially equal. Inequality must be stopped, inequality in status and inequality in property ownership. No more masters and servants, wives and maids, employers and employees, governments and subjects, for authority is presumptive despotism, obedience is slavery, submission is bondage, and service is groveling. Every organic, moral relationship that has existed so far must for the future be transformed into a contractual relationship: all service must become a position with a function. Similarly inequality in property may not continue; each person has equal rights and must receive as much as he deserves. In the future, people must no longer be able to be rich through a benefactor, through birth, or through inheritance, but rather wealth must be distributed strictly according to rights: every wage according to desert, or perhaps distribution according to need. This latter point has not yet been resolved.

It requires no argument that the ideal of such a society cannot be realized in any other way than by dismantling the existing society down to its foundations and then rebuilding it according to the specifications that have been dreamt up for a new society. Current society displays in every respect the greatest inequality and the richest diversity, far greater inequality and diversity than its opponents usually imagine. For they divide society actually into only two classes: the filthy rich and the dirt poor, the superpowerful and the powerless, the abusers and the abused, tyrants and slaves. But the real society, the society that lives and breathes, does not look at all like that; the diversity is far greater, so great that no one can form a complete picture of it. The filthy rich constitute a very small minority, and of these people, membership along a continuum proceeds down to the bottom not by a big leap but rather in terms of a gradual slope in various degrees and in various stages. Within society, there is not only an aristocratic class, but also an academic class, a merchant class, a manufacturing class, a middle class, a retail class, a skilled laboring class, and a laboring class. Among each of those classes there is again endless movement: there are large, average, and small merchants and retailers, and the number is by no means small of business owners who carry a far heavier load than many an employee and laborer. The misery of society is not that classes exist according to the vocations and enterprises that are practiced, but that the classes are forcibly turned upside down and that people who are torn from these social connections are then, contrary to all reality, divided into two classes, in terms of which only outward property, apart from all enterprise, serves as the measure.

Moreover, the fact that society displays such a textured diversity is not to be blamed on accident or arbitrariness, but flows from the nature of society itself. For the gifts and aptitudes in terms of soul and body that are bestowed upon people already at birth are unequal. Members of the family, from which society is built, are unequal in gender, age, and relationship. The forms of labor to which people devote their strength are unequal. Therefore the society that gradually comes into existence under the operation of all these factors is unequal. A society that is a genuine society, and as such is a complex organism of relationships and operations, cannot be anything but multiform. Just as the body is one yet has many members and all the members of this one body, being many, are one body, even so has the church of Christ been formed, according to the apostle Paul. And according to this law of organic life society has also been organized. So one who opposes the diversity of class and property in society thereby opposes its organic composition and must see to it that all organic, moral relationships are replaced by artificial, contractual relationships. And because the organization of society possesses its starting point and its stability in the family, the struggle against society ultimately leads to a struggle against the family, against the distinction and relationship of husband and wife, of parents and children, of those who are independent and those who are subservient.

Indeed, society is something other and something more than a collection of families. But that notwithstanding, within the various gifts and powers, relationships and activities that are distributed among the members of the family, lie embedded the principles of the complex order of society. Just as science extends the concepts implanted within human consciousness, just as technology strengthens the organs of the human body, so too society expands and develops the life of the family. The health of the family is a gauge, if not of society's material welfare, then certainly of its spiritual and moral well-being.

The Moral Character of All Labor and the Necessary Distinctions within Society

For by nature the man has a different disposition, different needs and inclinations, a different calling than the woman. No theory or law can erase this difference, which is grounded in creation. Whereas the wife finds her sphere of labor in the family, the man looks outward and there searches for an arena for his manpower. But in that connection it is very important that he is bound to the family by means of moral bonds. For if he were separated from the family and placed by himself, he would run the risk of losing sight of the moral seriousness of life, and of finding the purpose of his existence in selfish pleasure. The man who as head of the family enters his sphere of work in society and is bound by the bond of love to his wife and children, however, overcomes selfishness, living and working for others; the moral responsibility resting on his shoulders delivers him from many dangers. From the family he derives the moral drive for work, and he returns to his family with the fruits of this labor. Both being at home and being away from home keep each other in balance. In the man the moral bond is laid down between family and society; his work ties together the natural bonds of the family with the voluntary bonds of civil society.

With this, labor obtains simultaneously and immediately a moral character. In itself work is not a curse but a blessing, no shame but an honor, no compulsion but a calling and privilege. But if work is severed from its moral principle and its moral purpose, it quickly becomes a heavy burden, or a means of indulgence. Presently here on earth, work is paired with difficulty; it must be done in the sweat of one's brow, not only by the manual laborer who works with his body, but also by the craftsman and the salesman, the teacher and the thinker, who work especially with their mind. What a monotonous boredom characterizes many a job; what objections and difficulties must be conquered day after day; what patience and self-denial, what spiritual strength and effort are demanded to keep shouldering the burden, to avoid sticking one's hands in his pockets from discouragement; and above all, what a cheerfulness of spirit is needed in order to move forward joyfully and gratefully, as one should, to create delight and joy in one's work! How many today complain as they work and view it merely as a means for earning money, or simply as a means enabling them to enjoy life as much as possible later in the evening and at night, on Sunday and holidays!

This is in fact a regression to the position of Greek antiquity, when work was viewed as a disgrace and a task for slaves. But Christianity has taught us differently. Christ himself has sanctified work by his life and suffering. He has made us understand that work is a moral calling, a calling that comes to us from God and that must be fulfilled for his sake. The purpose of work is inherent neither in work itself nor in pleasure nor in wealth. "Those who desire to be rich fall into temptation, into a snare, into many senseless and harmful desires that plunge people into ruin and destruction" (1 Tim. 6:9). These words of Paul apply still today; indeed, it's as though they were written with a view to our social circumstances. Anyone who abstracts work from the moral context in which God placed it debases work and robs work of its honor. Work, all work, including the least and most simple, is once again a source of joy only when we see it as a divine calling that has been assigned to us as our task here on earth. And that moral calling of work does not hover above us in the air and is no abstract theory, but lies embedded in life itself, in the family. Through the family God motivates us to work, inspiring, encouraging, and empowering us to work. Through this labor he equips us to survive not for the sake of satisfying our lusts but for the sake of providing for our family before God and with honor, and also to extend the hand of Christian compassion to the poor.

This moral character of work must be emphasized the more strongly since, in our time, work is undergoing all kinds of important changes. Technology has now been elevated to the rank of a science, and has gradually turned man into a ruler of nature and of all its powers. Every invention that he makes is a kind of emancipation; steam and electricity shortened the distances and render people more and more independent of place and time, of wind and weather. But with this liberation from the power of nature, the social dependence of people has not decreased, but quite the opposite, it has increased to a large degree. In the patriarchal period each family was, as it were, its own society; because the family itself supplied all its needs through its own manpower, it did not need the produce of the labor of others and enjoyed a great measure of independence. But in the course of time this has changed completely. Labor is now divided and distributed to an endless degree and has given rise to an incalculable number of independent enterprises: there are separate vocations for clothier and cobbler, for carpenter and mason, for baking and butchering, for trading and selling, for teaching and learning, for practicing the sciences and the arts, and all these kinds of work have their own subspecialties and have given rise to a platoon of specialties and experts.

Technology assists this division of labor, and gradually increases the distance between employer and employee, on the one hand, and that between producer and consumer, on the other hand. For as a result of the cost of the means of production (tools and machinery), the production of goods within many enterprises is being turned over more frequently to other companies that work for corporations run by a director and employing hundreds of workers who, having been robbed of all means of production, have retained only their manpower. Similarly, the expansion of travel and trade enables the producer to import his raw materials from all around the world, and to seek a market for the products of labor in the remotest countries and the most diverse nations. An inestimable number of people in various parts of the world have been working to produce the food and drink we enjoy, the clothes we wear, the houses in which we live, all the small and big things that supply our manifold needs. To a stronger degree than ever before, people and nations have become socially and economically dependent on each other. A strategically organized strike can rob an entire world-class city in one instant of light and water, and shut down all traffic into and out of the city. This is how at the present time society has become a composite of the most manifold and complex relationships. Those relationships lose more and more of their personal, organic, moral character, and shift toward mechanical, business, contractual networks.

One must of course beware of harmful exaggeration in this connection. Not one of the somber prophecies uttered by the leaders of socialism concerning the development of society has come to pass. The industrial revolution has been accompanied not by a decrease but an increase in the number of businesses. The consolidation of businesses did not interfere with agriculture, nor gain the momentum in industry that socialism had predicted. Although in some branches of business, such as the mining industry, for example, large companies grew larger, in other areas the average size and smaller companies not only survived but even expanded; manual labor came into its own again, and the number of jobs increased. There has not been a consolidation of capital and land; although there are a few immensely wealthy people, alongside large incomes smaller and average incomes are growing as well; there is a general expansion of capital and prosperity, the number of property owners is increasing, and more people than previously are enjoying the increasing production of goods. Laborers are not unhappier than previously, but are advancing in terms of lifestyle, living standard, and development; the labor of women and children is restricted by law in many countries, and the theory that workers would have become more and more miserable is strongly contradicted by the facts that many people who initially accepted it later abandoned it; Marxism yields to revisionism, and revolution yields to evolution.

The history of the last half century has brought to light so clearly that nothing is as dangerous as generalizing and lumping everything together. There is not a single law that governs the entire development of society; there is not simply one theory that fits all the facts of reality; all events do not move along a single straight line. Just as in previous centuries, society exhibits the richest diversity; that diversity itself has increased to a large extent through the progress of science and technology, of agricultural industry, of trade and traffic. It is not the case that two classes stand in opposition against each other—the rich and the poor, entrepreneurs and employees, the rulers and the oppressed. Instead, life is infinitely varied. In every enterprise, there are large and small, strong and weak, between whom again there exists not a gap but differences of degree. All those enterprises are not governed by one and the same protocol, but their operation depends on the country and people, on entrepreneurial spirit and ability, in order to grow in one direction or another. Modern society is no different in principle from previous ones and will not differ radically from the society of the future. The expectation that sooner or later a society will arise in which all misery will disappear and everyone will be equal is an illusion. The distinctions between men and women, parents and children, government and citizens, employers and employees, rich and poor, healthy and sick, will always exist. There is no power in the world able to alter these natural ordinances.

Abuses and the Path toward Improvement

Nevertheless with all of this we are not saying that in various respects the present society is not exhibiting its own unique shape and is not moving generally in a socializing direction. For example, the state is expanding its activities further and further in the area of protecting material interests, and has assumed the maintenance of roads and waterways, postal and telegraph service, shipping and train service, etc. The local municipal government maintains gas and water services, along with electricity, city transportation, and telephone services. An increasing consolidation has occurred in various businesses, and public limited companies, cooperative associations, and employment unions continually increase in significance. Whereas in previous centuries each city and each corporation had its own rights, now virtually all the people are included in the one great world- and trade-movement. We are seeing a universal pursuit of equality, a yearning to eliminate all distinction based on birth or property and not on personal value, a strong push for independence and freedom. In church and state, in family and society, in vocation and business, each person wants to see their own rights defined, wants to cast their own vote, and wants to stand up for their own interests.

In this pursuit there is much that we can accept as required by the times in which we live, much that we can appreciate as completely legitimate. In the name of Christianity we cannot disapprove of much of this, for this religion, more than any other religion or ethics, has highlighted the value of the human personality. The human soul is more valuable than the whole world. But this pursuit may enjoy our sympathy and support—and can work beneficially—only to the degree that it is directed by religious-moral principles and is guided by the law of God. The person who pursues simply and only independence ends up glorifying the will to power, the right of the strongest; and because such anarchy cannot be tolerated, he is one day reined in by someone stronger or forcibly put in chains by society itself. The individual and the community can live in peace, even as husband and wife, parents and children, government and citizens, employer and worker, only if a moral authority stands over them, defining the rights and duties of both and guarding the interests of each.

And that in fact is the case. The individual person is not free; he cannot do what he wants. He is not only limited by his environment, but he also senses that he is bound by his conscience and is responsible for his thoughts, desires, and actions. Similarly, society is not sovereign and almighty, but bound to ordinances that God has established for it. For society itself is grounded in moral principles. Indeed, people committed to a materialist or socialist viewpoint have supposed that society with all its relationships and goods should be a product of economic, material circumstances. But this teaching directly contradicts reality. Even though society exerts influence on its members, society itself is always composed of people who come not only with a body and a stomach, but also with a heart and a soul, an intellect and a conscience. No matter what interests may induce people to form a connection with each other, these are always people who are morally responsible and may not do whatever they may happen to desire or want. Sometimes, in fact, such connections are formed with a view to protecting spiritual and moral interests, such as, for example, science, art, charity, compassion, etc.

But even if it involves purely material interests, like developing a mine, cultivating the soil, producing various material goods, etc., then still these always involve people who are in a particular relationship with each other, who respect each other as people, and who are subject to a common law for all their thinking and acting. Before anything else, a society is a complex composite of *moral* relationships. It matters very little if these moral relationships are incorporated into the law as legal regulations; occasionally codifying a right is proof that such moral relationships no longer possess adequate security in people's consciences. But from their very origin, they rest in the spiritual, moral nature of the human person and their ultimate firm footing lies there; a law that is not rooted in conscience is powerless; a people's economy is based on their ethics.

If this indeed is the case, then once again we see the extraordinary significance that the family possesses for the moral well-being of society. For there in the family from the moment we enter the world we get to know all those relationships that we will enter later in society—relationships of freedom and connectedness, independence and dependence, authority and obedience, equality and difference. And we get to know them in the family not in an abstract academic way, not by theoretical instruction, but practically, in and through life itself; all moral relationships are embedded and interwoven in the family, in the bonds of blood, and they are rooted in the origins of human existence. In the family we get to know the secret of life, the secret, namely, that not selfishness but self-denial and self-sacrifice, dedication and love, constitute the rich content of human living.

And from the family we carry those moral relationships into society. One who has learned to honor his father later respects the authority of those through whom it has pleased God to rule over him. One who has truly loved his mother cannot violate another woman's honor. One who views the family servants as housemates cannot become a tyrant over his own employees. The family is the nursery of love and inoculates society with such love.

We need that love if there is going to be any reform within society. Not selfishness, not greed, not thirst for domineering, but love is the foundation and the cement of the Christian society. Christianity is not the architect, but the soul of society. One who destroys the family is digging away the moral foundations on which society has been established as a moral institution. But one who exalts the family and outfits leadership with love rather than selfishness, such a person does a work that pleases God. For God is love and love is the law of his kingdom.

10

THE FUTURE OF THE FAMILY

Changes in the Family

If the moral health of society depends on the health of family life, the question is of interest whether the attempt to guard and restore the family has any chance for success. There are not a few who see the struggle for the family as hopeless and abandon it in advance because they think that evolution, to which today's society is subject, will lead inevitably to the dissolution and destruction of family life of a prior period. Indeed, there are many phenomena indicating that the ancient patriarchal family is undergoing a severe crisis and an important reformation.

In earlier times, when the sense of family was much stronger, the family constituted one independent, enclosed entity. Husband and wife, parents and children, male and female slaves, house and land, sometimes even grandparents and grandchildren, together constituted the home and family. At the head of the family stood the father who was master of everyone and everything. That is not to say that wife and children were his property in the same sense as his slaves and his livestock, his house or his garden; but the man was nevertheless the head, the master, the owner, and the maintainer of the great entity of the family. In earliest times, when there was yet no state or church, he was king and priest, lawgiver and judge, in his home. This family community was so strong that when the man died, no separation and splitting up of property occurred among the children; rather, all his authority and all the family's property went undivided to the oldest son, the firstborn son, who for that reason enjoyed significant privileges beyond all the other children. Gradually these rights of the family became limited, through the state or the church, through government and jurisprudence. But in various countries the ancient situation still continues in this form, such that the inheritance of the family property, of the family house and land, is transferred only to the eldest son, while the younger brothers and sisters must be satisfied with a small distribution, and must provide for themselves.

The development of society has made a far greater encroachment upon the family. For whereas in previous times each family provided for virtually all of its own needs, including its own food and drink, covering and clothing, dwelling and furnishings, such that people went to the city or to the market at most several times a year to purchase some housekeeping goods and tools, nowadays baking and cooking, weaving and tailoring, the work of carpentry and masonry, have all become independent enterprises. In remote regions the ancient pattern continues; but in the cities and villages, where the cultural life of the modern era has penetrated, the family has virtually lost its economic independence entirely, and has become dependent on its surrounding society for the provision of all of its needs. In addition, in the cities the idea of a parental home and of one's own dwelling is slowly losing its importance. Personal inheritance is a thing of the past; thousands of families have completely lost touch with any experience of owning property and of property rights. They live permanently in rented dwellings and they relocate frequently; their children must often leave home at an early age to get training for this or that job and eventually to

The Future of the Family

earn their own living; often their possessions consist of little more than a few articles of personal property that are often disposed and replaced, holding little sentimental value. Gradually the family is losing its natural foundation and emotional unity. It has been said, not without justification, that the countryside is the natural sphere of the family, but the city is the natural enemy of the family.

Yet all of this is not the worst of it. The entirety of modern life is a power that fragments and reduces the family. Work so preoccupies the husband and sometimes the wife as well, along with the children, that they return home in the evening late and tired, only to leave home again early the next morning. There is no time and no desire left over for conviviality, for cultivating a sense of family, for nurturing the children. Even Sunday has become a workday for thousands of families, or a day for getting out that leaves them no less exhausted. The houses where husband, wife, and children must live in the countryside and in the cities are often so miserable that they lack any coziness and attractiveness, and serve mostly as a place to spend the night. The activities of various clubs and groups, designed for relaxation and fun, or for engaging various political and social interests, have expanded so widely that in a very troubling way these also promote being away from home. Many a husband and wife come home after a full day's work only to eat, leaving immediately to attend a meeting or gathering, a club or social event, until late in the evening and far into the night. This notion of socializing that one breathes with the air leads to the question whether it is not a useless waste of time and money for each family to have its own kitchen and cooking stove, to prepare its own food and serve its own meals. Effort and expenses could be reduced if a central cooking stove and a communal kitchen were to provide for the needs of a large number of residences.

In reality, holiday meals are more frequently being held out of people's homes in hotels and restaurants. In Berlin people are already building barracks-like dwellings that house many families under one roof, with one central furnace and a communal kitchen for their meals. This socializing of the family is facilitated in turn by what is called the "housekeepers' plague." Many a young woman, upon entering her new home with her husband and with a heart filled with ideals, quickly lost all her illusions when she encountered reality and discovered how hard it is to be responsible for the housekeeping. The complaints regarding women and housekeepers did not arise for the first time in the modern era; they are as old as the world. But today they are being sounded more loudly because, on the one hand, women are being trained much more with a view to other things than for housekeeping, and on the other hand, housekeepers are pursuing a different social position and want to identify their service more in terms of a professional position.

The most serious dangers are threatening the family, however, from the side of new theories regarding marriage and family life. Today both are viewed by many as an antiquated form of living together. In their opinion, the anticipated new society brings with it a new religion and a new ethic. According to this new ethic, no other law exists for the union of man and woman than open love, unrestrained blind passion. A man and a woman commit themselves arbitrarily, without needing to take into consideration church or state, God or his commandment. They come together and they leave each other strictly as the desire of their heart inclines them. No longer does that commitment at all entail having children and raising those children to be citizens of the kingdom of God or even to be good citizens of the state. For procreation is entirely within their power; they decide that matter in terms of their own well-being. If it suits them, they will have children; but if they judge differently, then they simply decline to have children, or they arbitrarily limit the number of children, and they choose to destroy life in the womb. Nature cannot be changed which places on the woman the burden of motherhood and obligates her to care for the child for some time after birth; but once they are weaned, all the children come under the auspices of the state, and the state must be happy that it is receiving so much power for nothing in exchange, and the children need merely to be raised in one school and according to a uniform model.

For the ideal that must be realized is equality; the woman must be relieved as much as possible from the burdens of motherhood and from the servitude of the home. She ought to enjoy the same rights and duties as the man, and to participate in the same privileges of citizenship. The state is the one true family, and all the citizens are members of that family with equal rights. These theories are gradually making their way out of the academy into the practice of life itself. There is nothing to be done, as someone recently stated, since antiquated marriage can no longer be maintained; evolution is quietly and unnoticeably paving the way for open marriages and open love. In reality, such emancipation is progressing further and further; the number of births is declining in almost all civilized countries, especially in France and the United States of America; divorce is increasing at an alarming rate, and is being made more easy through legislation and judicial action; sexual activity is casting off one restraint after another.

Protecting the Family against Such Changes

Nevertheless, no matter how gloomy all of this may be and no matter the effort it may take to row against the current of the age, Christians may not permit their conduct to be determined by the spirit of the age, but must focus on the requirement of God's commandment. Even if they come to stand alone, as history has so often obligated them to do, they must show in word and deed what an inestimable blessing God has granted to humanity and to society, to church and state, with the gift of marriage and family. But they may also be encouraged by knowing that the struggle for the honor and welfare of the family is a noble struggle that carries with it the promise of victory. Not for nothing has God permitted the continuation of the family in the human race and among all peoples; every family ever built and every child ever born is proof that his purpose with the human race has not yet been achieved, that his forbearance has not yet ended, and his grace has not yet been exhausted. For that reason, life is never as consistent as logic would require the theory to be. Life does not always follow a straight line of deterioration, but often comes to a pause and even a reversal. An ebb tide follows a surge; action spurs reaction; dissoluteness generates again the need for power and authority.

So it is completely false to view history as a process of evolution where everything moves involuntarily and powerlessly. In many respects the human person might well be dependent on his environment, and might be determined by nature, birth, nurture, etc. in his thinking and acting. Nevertheless, he is more than a product of society; he is a unique, independent personality, and from his position he affects his environment through the exercise of his will. The human will, especially when it is guided by reason and conscience, by the Word and command of God, is not impotent, but represents an insuperable power in the world. It places restraints on nature, suppresses passions, and reforms society. People cannot create anything, the foundations of society were laid once and for all by God himself; but on those foundations people can build further and restore what needs restoring. So we may never despair of the reformation of human beings and family and society. Even if modern man should doubt its possibility, the Christian may not surrender to this discouragement, because genuine piety holds promise for this life and for the life to come.

So in contrast to the negative side of contemporary society there is also a positive side. It is interesting that many eyes have been opened to the dangers to which the family is exposed, and that from all sides powerful attempts are being undertaken to protect family life and preserve it from shipwreck. In all countries and among various schools of thought, men and women have arisen and joined together to form organizations whose purpose is, through reform of education and of childcare, to prepare children for their future, to safeguard children and adolescents from temptation, to restrain married men from their sinful ways, to protect the honor of women, to oppose all forms of slave trade, to restrict the houses of ill repute, to seek the lost, to rescue the fallen, to offer support and help to unmarried mothers and orphans. No matter how stimulating it may be, here is not the place to describe or to summarize all of what has been initiated and is being done in this area. But the claim of Wichern[1] has been echoed in the hearts of many: we need a reformation, or better, a revival of all our inner affections by means of new and renewed deeds of faith and love. The church of Christ ought to understand that her gift and her calling include not faith alone, but also love.

The work of this protecting and rescuing love is not, as some have thought, pushed into the background or even rendered superfluous by the social and political activity undertaken in recent years. Outward improvement, as desirable as it may be, is something entirely different than inward renewal. For this latter, all social and political reformation is unequipped. The state is not the sphere of love but of justice; it does not proclaim the gospel but enforces the law. For that reason, the state can never take over or displace the task of the family; the state is not a parent who provides its citizens with food and clothing and a place to live, with work and wages, sustenance and pension. The state presupposes the family, as does society, both of which existed before the state, each leading their own lives and being governed by their own laws. Anyone who expects the state to satisfy all those interests, for which family and society and church are to look after, is undermining the independence of these spheres of life and is calling for a remedy that in the long run will turn out to be more dangerous than the disease.

But whereas the state must respect the freedom and uniqueness of these spheres of life, the state itself has a special and lofty calling. As minster of God, the government must see to it that the rights of family and society, or each citizen and each sphere, are acknowledged and protected, and in case of conflict, ensure that justice is maintained. Consequently the state must call into being all such universal conditions whereby all citizens can fulfill their

---

1 Ed. note: J. H. Wichern (1808–81) was a German theologian and prison reformer.

particular task and can answer to their own destiny in the sphere in which God has placed them and in agreement with the commandment he has given them. From this flow unique obligations that the government must perform with respect to the family. The state can neither create nor maintain the family, the state need not arrogantly constitute the family through law, and even less may it oppress and oppose the family.

The task of the state is to discover the internal law to which the family is subject by virtue of its nature and the ordinance established by God, to acknowledge, protect, and maintain this law. In this way, by means of its legislation regarding marriage and divorce, property and inheritance, working hours and Sunday rest, the labor of women and children, public decency and many other things, the state would be working in a powerful way for the well-being and flourishing of the family. The state's ideal is not to do everything itself, but to provide every citizen and all the spheres of life in society with the opportunity for each in their own domain to fulfill their own calling.

Today the government is aware, at least in part, of this task of protecting the family. Even in radical and socialist circles, where people would not expect, in recent times voices have arisen pleading for the enhancement of the family. For years, Marx and his disciples have championed the idea that the development of the capitalist society would continually suppress wages, would give rise to more women and children working, and in that way the family would gradually dissolve and be destroyed. People then expected that further along this route, women would achieve their grand liberation as they were included as instruments of labor within enormous industries. For if in this immense industrial society she was made equal to men in an economic sense, then she would win the same rights in society that men had enjoyed already for a long time. Women would move from the previous "home servitude" through current "wage servitude" to obtain in the society of the future her full independence, not only from men and housekeeping, but also from her children. For already within a relatively short time after birth, these children are handed over for their communal rearing on behalf of the state. And after the obligatory day job, they would receive, just like men, the opportunity to devote themselves to those activities that they would find most enjoyable.

But the evolution of society has not fulfilled this expectation of socialism. Wages have not gone down but have risen; the labor of women and children has not expanded but contracted; and even in the circles of socialists, the woman has retained her nature and the mother her love for her children. In this way division has arisen among the disciples of Marx regarding the question whether one should have targeted the complete emancipation of the woman from the so-called slavery of men, homemaking, and children, or whether the pursuit should have focused on returning the woman in the future more and more to the family. The latter sentiment has even been enjoying a powerful defense. Socialist men have also declared decisively and unapologetically that the first duty of the woman is to live for her family; that the so-called women's liberation conflicts entirely with her feminine nature; and that in the future society as well, even though the production of goods will have become a communal matter, the family and family life must continue to exist.

The Continuation of Family Life

So then, the facts teach something entirely different than that evolution necessarily entails or includes the dissolution of the family. The family is indeed threatened by serious dangers and is exposed to all kinds of opposition, but it is our duty to review these dangers and our calling to resist in a powerful way every hostile force that undermines the foundation of the family. It cannot be denied that home life is undergoing many noteworthy changes at present. Just as in broader society, privilege and rank, birth and nobility, are more and more losing their significance and giving way to the personal worth of the individual, so too in family life each member is reaching personal independence and freedom far earlier and energetically than before. The ancient patriarchal family is developing more and more into a modern family, one that has become disconnected from nature and location, from soil and land, and from the entire feudal regime. One may regret this in many respects, but the current cannot be resisted, since the development is moving in the direction of personal freedom.

The authority of the husband is increasingly adopting a more reasonable and moral character. The woman has been freed by the new organization of society from various kinds of work that she performed previously, and thus has greater need for a wider field of vision and circle of activity. At present children must stand on their own and make their own way in life much earlier than before. Housekeepers pursue changing their job into a professional position. Everything currently depends far more on what a person himself is and becomes and does than on the family or class to which one belongs by nature.

But one may not deduce from all of this that the family is disappearing and family life will be destroyed. The forms may change, but the essence remains. Whatever changes the new society may bring about, human nature remains the same everywhere. Man and woman differ now, and in the future will differ just as much as previously in physical and psychological constitution, in disposition, capacity, and life calling. One can indeed talk about servitude at home and about male tyranny, and can portray the woman as being genuinely free only when she achieves economic independence. But 90 percent of women still always opt for that home servitude far rather than working in this or that company. It sounds nice to say that the woman must also have time to devote herself to art and science. But this destiny remains open merely for a few women in any case. If women wanted to achieve economic independence, they would need to enter all those professions that are currently being performed by men. And those professions are rarely as desirable as they are often presented; in terms of monotonous, troublesome, and boring activity, they are truly not superior to the work of the woman in the family.

When it comes to bottom line, the woman can nowhere land in a better situation than in the family, at the side of a husband who loves her, surrounded by her children whom she tends and nurtures. Her nature is designed for that, her orientation lies in that direction, there she best fulfills her calling and best reaches her destiny. There is then no more foolish requirement and no more unnatural compulsion than to propose to the wife that in the coming political state, she must give up her children, once they're weaned, to the community. The mother for whom maternal love is the unspeakable mystery and inexhaustible power in her life will never allow herself to be separated from her children in this way; she desires not merely to give them birth, but also to raise them, and she remains bound to them until the hour of her death.

The natural and spiritual bonds between husband and wife, like those between parents and children, are stronger than the utopian theories constructed about human society. They are more strengthened than weakened by the recent development of society. Perhaps there are families here and there that, among other things, in order to be spared the worry of servants have taken up living or eating in hotels; but by the nature of the case those are exceptions that could never become the norm. Here and there people have begun to organize living in barracks-like dwellings with one communal kitchen. But it remains a question whether this experiment will succeed and find sympathy among very many. It will likely remain an experiment; just as marriage and family require their own room or dwelling, so too as a rule private houses cannot lack their own kitchens. But even if such a communal kitchen might become common for a smaller or larger group of families in a few cities, that would not affect the essence of family life, as though this were comparable to various forms of the socializing of labor, like proponents of the new society are suggesting. Today that same work that previously occurred is hardly any longer being performed in the family. Today the wife no longer needs to be busy with spinning and weaving, washing and ironing, making clothes and baking bread, as in former days every family had to provide for its own needs in that way; water and light are supplied today in every locale of any size by means of residential community service to every family.

All of this had been to the greater advantage of family life, rather than harming family life. For while the bond of the family with nature has become more loose, the bond between family members together has gained strength. The wife needs to perform less work in connection with the actual housekeeping; but the greater convenience and cleanliness that home life requires today, and especially the more expanded physical and spiritual care of the children, occupy her time and energy that much more. In general the rise in wages and in living standard, the restrictions on the labor of women and children, serve to reinvigorate the family. If the future development of society can take this approach, that the woman need not supplement the family's earnings, because the income of the husband would be adequate, then women in general would not go looking for employment in society, but instead return with deep gratitude and love to their families.

On top of all this we have the remarkable phenomenon that we are seeing a rather significant retreat from the city to the country. For years on end, the countryside was being depopulated and large numbers were moving to the cities; there they could find both work and enjoyments in abundance. But the fat years are gone and they have left behind various kinds of disappointment and dissatisfaction; in the cities poverty is far greater than in the countryside, and unemployment is a constantly recurring, extremely discouraging phenomenon. The demands that modern civilization places on the cities makes living more expensive and causes taxes to rise, almost by the year. The houses are often small and uncomfortable, deprived of sunlight and fresh air. There is far less conviviality in the cities than in smaller places; not without justification, the large cities have been called conviviality's graveyard.

In the face of all those negative elements, the positive elements begin to disappear; even the enjoyments that are available are often impure and leave a huge hole in the heart. In this way a desire has gradually awakened for the tranquility and peace of country living; people want to leave the busyness, the bustle, the constant motion of the large cities in order to find oneself again, to taste that quiet delight that only nature and the family circle can provide. It is once again sensed as a lack when in the city people are always sitting between walls, never able to enjoy the wide open spaces and the fresh air of land and sea. By means of city parks and playgrounds people try to provide somewhat for that need of being close to nature; for children's vacation, for the sick and weak and elderly, people look in the countryside for a place of retreat and renewal. Industrial entrepreneurs build their factories, and employees look for their houses, outside the city limits; aristocratic families build or rent their country homes and villas for part or all of the year.

In those homes people yearn again for a unique style and unique furnishings. The monotony and uniformity of modern life gets to be so boring that people sigh with deep longing for originality in art. People have enough of the overwhelming ornamentation, and they thirst again for authenticity. The oversaturation of culture arouses a hunger for nature. The city becomes more and more a "business place," where people in a big hurry do their business only to flee as quickly as they can to get outside for fresh air, for renewal and enjoyment, tranquil and deep. Individualism resists socialism from all sides. Marx has made way for Nietzsche.[2]

Changes Relating to Servants

In addition, the changes occurring in the employment and training of girls, and in the matter of private property, do not point to a dissolution of the family. The domestic servants are quite

---

[2] Ed. note: Bavinck's point is that the city is meant to be the communal ideal, but instead it leads to a lack of conviviality whereas true meaning is sought in the country, implying that city life actually promotes individualism and a general absence of meaning, peace, and tranquility, i.e. nihilism, as Nietzsche made popular through his writings.

self-aware, and they present their mistresses with an extended list of demands. Even though many times this may well be awkward and unpleasant, nevertheless in the abstract no one denies the reasonableness and fairness of all those demands. Here as well one must guard against generalizations; there have always been good and bad housewives, and good and bad servants as well; the work is more pleasant and favorable in one family than in another, and one servant differs significantly from another in terms of suitability and serviceability. Socialism has no eye for all these differences in the life of society, since it recognizes only two classes; on the one side are the housewives, who are always rich and tyrannical, and on the other side are the domestic servants, who are always poor and miserable slaves. By means of this untruthful contrast, socialism causes a lot of evil, inciting women and domestic servants more and more against each other, and socialism tempts some people to adopt an entirely opposite position, excusing the women from all blame and casting it on the domestic servants.

But that is just as one-sided; we must admit forthrightly that in many cases, domestic servants have a right to complain, and may legitimately appeal for a higher wage, more free time, better housing conditions, and more friendly treatment. Housewives must take this into account and must fulfill legitimate demands, preferably not first through coercion but on their own, by virtue of their Christian calling; and if the work gradually obtains the character of a contractual relationship, then they need to adjust to the circumstances and get used to the new situation. Along with the disappearance of the former relationship, often many lovely and heartwarming features that characterized the concourse between women and domestic servants will also be lost. But the patriarchal family is gone, and the new arrangement is advantageous for the intimacy of the family and for the elevation of those who provide services.

Even if the domestic servants were to go so far that, like the young ladies in an office or in a store, they would be able to come for specified hours during the day to do their work in a home, then that would have the simple result that the family would constitute a smaller and still more intimate circle. The old notion that the family consisted of many more other persons than the parents and the children would disappear entirely, but the bond of marriage and kinship would be strengthened more tightly and the sense of spiritual togetherness would be strengthened by this as well. On the other side, with this new arrangement the domestic servants will certainly gain more independence, freedom, and personal development; but the "employment relationship" into which the domestic servant wishes to transition her work will undoubtedly grant the right to her employer to set higher demands than previously, and that work will essentially continue to have the character of a job for the domestic servant.

One must not forget that at present, the family is often a school for the domestic servants, where they themselves are trained in home life. Not infrequently they begin their job without any ability and need to be introduced by the housewives with much patience and wisdom into the many little secrets of housekeeping and cooking. But if from the side of the domestic servants, the work acquires more and more the character of employment, then whether or not they want this, they will automatically increase the expectations that are tied to fulfilling such employment. Perhaps it will go as far as negotiating the requirement for entering this job of having a diploma from a school teaching the skills of housekeeping and cooking; why should domestic servants remain exempt from the rule that obtains in the world of employment, namely, that they be examined?

But no matter how this development may unfold, the employment relationship whereby the domestic servants come for a specified number of hours in a day to perform their contracted work for a fixed wage would not injure family life, and by itself would always continue to exhibit the character of a job. And that is what domestic servants must continue to remember, with all the reforms that they advocate. Arrange it so that each morning they need not begin their work before a set time, and so that they may finish at a similarly fixed time in the afternoon or evening, and in that way receive far more free time than formerly; during the time when they are fulfilling their employment, they are and remain in service. There is no reform imaginable whereby this work relationship would change; anyone who claims differently is living in a fantasy world, though perhaps with good intentions. During the days and hours of employment, the relationship between masters and servants, between mistresses and maids, remains *essentially* the same as Scripture portrays it. Like the manager in the factory, the businessman in the office, the salesman in the store, etc., the wife in the family remains in charge of her domestic servants.

Naturally, within all these life spheres, the authority changes in terms of the nature of the relationship, but in terms of its essence it continues to exist in all of them. Within the family, authority over the housekeeping rests with the woman and not with the servants. That is not only her right, but also her duty. It is the calling of the woman to supervise all the housekeeping, including the kitchen, to strongly combat every form of quarreling, dishonesty, and thievery, and to maintain order in terms of the thousand details of life, all of which can be a rich blessing for the subsequent life of the servant if she herself gets married. So the domestic servants may in general appeal for improvements in their status; but they must openly and honestly acknowledge this inalienable right of the mistress to manage her own housekeeping. The welfare of the family, including the servant's family, depends on that.

If the reform being sought in the world of domestic servants might result in the woman once again being thoroughly committed to this as her right and especially to this as her *obligation*, then family life would derive significant advantage from that. Currently the woman getting married is not infrequently completely unequipped for housework; because of her incompetence she is led by the nose by her domestic servant; in order to avoid unpleasant confrontations, she leaves everything in the kitchen and occasionally all the housework in the hands of her hired servant; every bond becomes torn, and the housewife and servant go their separate ways, to the harm of both of them and of all of home life. Authority is undermined from two sides; the mistress cannot maintain it because she lacks the requisite knowledge, and the domestic servant does not respect it because it is not paired with understanding; so for those few times when it is exercised, it displays a capricious character. Authority is not tyranny, either in the family or in society. The mistress who wants to maintain her authority with regard to housekeeping must in the first place be informed about it herself; her authority must be paired with knowledge, wisdom, and direction. She must be a mistress in the good, ancient sense of the word; then her administration will be an invaluable blessing for husband and children, for all the household and also for her domestic servants.

Changes in the Training of Girls

For that reason, very significant attention is currently being devoted to the training of the wife, and rightly so. In a former time this was largely or entirely neglected, but nowadays it has been placed in the forefront in every country. What can be observed in every sphere of society can be spotted also in the arena of women: a powerful striving for freedom and independence has been awakened. The woman, who often has been pushed all too much into the background, has acquired self-awareness and is demanding a place for herself in society, if not in the place of man then certainly as one with equal right alongside the man. Everywhere the number of women working outside their own families in professions and businesses is increasing almost annually. From the lower classes of society women are applying to work in factories as soon as the law permits, and prefer that above the less lucrative work in the family. Women from the small middle class seek jobs in teaching, nursing, postal work, telegraph service, public train transportation, in offices, at desks, and in stores. From the more prosperous circles many women prepare for a profession in science or art. And the demand continues to resound more loudly that all professions, businesses, and positions, together with all the schools serving to train for them, be opened just as widely and easily for women as they are for men. This has gone so far that not a few are claiming that this conflict will never end until women are placed on the same level as men in all respects in family and society, in church and state, socially, politically, and economically.

Among the feminists themselves, however, there exists no small difference. Some will not shrink back from any implication and register the demand that marriage and family as we know them today would disappear in the future. Others are more moderate, traveling the path not of revolution but of evolution, hoping that the woman's freedom and equality might come about within the boundaries of marriage and family. Among the women looking for a job, the number is very large of those who acknowledge that the woman does actually find her vocation within marriage and the family, in nurturing children and administering the housekeeping, but who, because in the current society they cannot count on that kind of future, choose for certainty over uncertainty and attempt to tread their own way through life. These latter have a legitimate claim upon our sympathy and support.

The actual hardcore feminists are few in number; their zeal for the political and economic equality of women with men finds very weak support among married women; if the law would grant suffrage to women, the result would be that most women would abstain from voting, even as in fact thousands of men already do. The women preparing for a profession in science and art constitute a relatively small number, and it is not likely that they will push the men out or provide them with any damaging competition. But the great difficulty with the women's issue lies with those many young ladies from the middle class who would like to marry but cannot, and therefore are seeking an arena of activity in society. For these young ladies it is unbearably difficult not to be permitted to declare what is their heart's wish, to feel unneeded in their parental home, to receive repeatedly from their entire surroundings the impression that they could just as easily be missed, and then to have to wait passively to see whether anyone comes to offer her his hand and thereby open for her a sphere of work within the family. It is understandable and legitimate that she would free herself from such a humiliating, hurtful dependence and would want to maintain her independence and her self-esteem in one or another form of employment. If one wishes to satisfy this explicable and legitimate longing, however, it remains desirable that, with the training of the young ladies as with the areas of work that become accessible to them, people continue taking into account the nature and disposition of women. This nature contains the principle that the wife be a suitable helper for her husband and a mother to her children. The woman who remains unmarried will thus be able to achieve her vocation and fulfill her calling best if she obtains the kind of employment that is connected as much as possible with family life. One can indeed seek the happiness of women in their political, social, and economic equality with men. But then one injures the nature of women, failing to distinguish between equality with men and identity with men, and society becomes more disintegrated than it already is now. The solution to the women's issue must be sought not in a diffuse distancing of women as far as possible from the family, but in an intentional return of women as much as possible to the family.

One may not forget that although the chances of marriage for many young ladies have become very uncertain, nevertheless in our country about 95 percent of women older than twenty get married, and most marriages by far are blessed with children. So theoretically and practically, women's vocation continues to lie with the family. However, when people train women in the same schools and for the same employment as men, then people are not taking into account either her nature or practical requirements. In that sense people are contributing to the disintegration of society, when later such women face an unexpected opportunity to marry, or seek to combine both employment and housekeeping—which in most cases is simply impossible; or for the sake of employment surrender marriage—which in most cases conflicts with the inclination of her heart; or, as usually occurs, without regret she gives up employment altogether along with her independence and freedom, and with great joy binds herself to the husband of her choosing. But in this latter case, with all her education she has not only wasted much time and money and work capacity, but also has acquired hardly any preparation for the huge task of housewife and mother.

These considerations lead to the conclusion that the young ladies must certainly desire another and better training than was formerly provided, but a training that as much as possible takes account of and relates to their nature and vocation.

In elementary school they receive the same instruction in the same school as the boys; this is entirely legitimate, because elementary school lays a communal foundation for the development of all citizens, and provides instruction in the years preceding puberty. But during the time when puberty occurs, separation is desirable. Coeducation, which has been recommended for a long time from various quarters, has not met the expectation; it is damaging to both parties. In the interest of their physical and emotional constitution, and with a view to their vocation, girls need a different education than boys. They must be prepared in ways that correspond with the requirement of their nature in terms of housekeeping, motherhood, caring for and nurturing their children. No matter what general formation people want to apply to them, which to a certain degree is proper, the woman's vocation may never be lost from view. Those few women who later decide to devote themselves to some profession or occupation may pursue their own course, but this small minority may not set the standard for the training of the large majority.

Even if some among this majority wish to prepare for employment in education, in postal service, in telegraph service, etc., for their sake as well training for family life may not be neglected. For ultimately this kind of training benefits those as well who are preparing for one or another job in society; not merely because many of them in fact get married, but also because as they live in an apartment or with a family, they render significant service for themselves and others, and can make themselves helpful in various respects and in various ways.

In this connection it is highly desirable that this knowledge of housekeeping not only be taught theoretically in school, by some instruction in principles of nurture, the art of cooking, etc., but also acquired practically in life, for example, by helping in institutions providing childcare, in orphanages, children's homes, etc. We are still far from seeing these desires fulfilled; there is still significant debate regarding the manner of organizing schools for girls. But in connection with the training of girls in terms of their vocation as wife and mother, there can be no doubt among those willing to take into account the direction people must generally follow with that training, for it begins with the feminine nature and its rootedness in practicality and in the demands of life.

At the present time, such training for housekeeping is needed for women since, as a result of various circumstances, the family itself cannot provide such training within the family, either at all or only deficiently or partially, and because the increased shortage of domestic servants creates a huge need for "lady servants," the kind of women from the aristocratic class who are forced to provide for their own maintenance, and who, taken in by another family, lend help in housekeeping there. In the future, along this route an arena for work will once again probably be closed for unmarried girls, which will lead them along another route back to the family, which in turn certainly deserves preference above many other jobs. But no matter how all of this may develop in the future, the solution of the women's issue lies generally and predominantly not in being separated from the family, but in returning to the family.

Changes in the Right of Property and Private Possessions

Finally, the development of the idea of property and private possessions does not lead inevitably and with irresistible logic to the dissolution of family life. They have certainly occasioned a remarkable change in this respect, one that has by no means reached its end. The patriarchal family possessed a communal house and land; its property consisted chiefly in natural goods, in slaves, land, livestock, means of subsistence, etc., and in later times as well slaves belonged to the estate on which they lived and with a change in ownership were transferred along with it. Today, however, money, which previously was only a medium of exchange and available in very limited quantity, has come to overshadow all other possessions; from being a medium of exchange, money has become the fruit and purpose of work; today people think of money when they think of capital.

This has occasioned a reversal in all social capacity and assets, in the entire range of social position and appreciation. Numerous families possess very little personal property any more, they own no parcel of land, no house, no yard, that they can call their property; their capital consists only in some clothes and furniture, in their wages paid to them weekly or monthly or yearly, and otherwise in stocks and shares. There is a negative side to be observed in this change in private property. With justification money is described as something without character. In itself money bears no moral quality and no moral purpose is tied to money. It can be used everywhere, as much for good as for evil, as much for advancing the kingdom of God as for supporting the kingdom of darkness; it can be used for all these by everybody, without distinction, by the best and the worst of people, and is not the least tied to intrinsic value, or personal, moral qualities. Not only that, but money falsifies values; it supplies someone who otherwise would have deserved and received the disregard of everyone an immediate social position honored by everyone, making him rise suddenly in rank and stature, in honor and renown. The proverb contains all too much truth that says: the coin that is round makes straight what is crooked and wise what is stupid. Money justifies everything.

Nevertheless, money is not inherently sinful; just like wisdom, money has acquired an ephemeral side for many people. That was the case already in the days of the Preacher of Ecclesiastes, but nowadays it is the case in a broader and deeper sense. For money has contributed in large measure to liberating man from his previous social dependence; money has made it possible that the efforts of parents do not benefit the firstborn son exclusively, but can be divided equally among the children; that slaves could be freed from the land on which they lived; that workers could become independent of their masters, could relocate at virtually any moment, and enter the employ of another boss; that trade could expand across the entire globe; in a word, that man could become much more independent over against nature.

In addition, to money we owe the fact that capital can be spread across a much larger number of people and families than in previous centuries. Indeed, socialism argues that capital would be consolidated more and more in the hands of a few, but the facts have contradicted this prophecy. On the contrary, as social capital increases, it too is spread across an increasing number of owners; it does not stay with a few magnates, but trickles down into continually lower and wider circles; the number of aristocratic citizens does not decrease, but rises; even among laborers wages have climbed and the living standard has risen; compared to previous times, the welfare, convenience, and enjoyment of life have increased in an extraordinary way among all ranks and classes of society.

Finally, by means of money the possibilities and opportunities are multiplied for all people to be active for the benefit of society. Surely the chance is increased in the same measure to abuse money; mammonism, greed, and covetousness are serious maladies in our present time. One can make money his god, and through money make his stomach his god. But that very same money also puts one in a position to support important undertakings through donations of a smaller or larger amount, and to further the work of culture; by means of small or large contributions to work together for the moral elevation of society, for the flourishing of churches and schools, for rendering various acts of mercy, for advancing the kingdom of God. Nowadays that is not a privilege reserved only for a few who are rich, but almost everyone can participate at present, each in his own way and according to the capacity granted to him.

In this connection, it comes down more to the quality than quantity of the gifts. For the natural man, money possesses only a quantitative value. But God accounts differently. He does not separate money from the moral quality of its owner; he demands an accounting of all the capacities over which he has appointed us stewards. In his eyes the widow's mite is more valuable than the gift flowing from a person's abundance, because it embodies self-sacrifice and he himself attaches his blessing to that. Thus for the Christian there exists no right at all to despise money or to criticize capital. Sin resides in the person, not in money; money is a good gift of God and affords opportunity for beneficial work.

The entire development that private property has undergone in recent centuries, however, points in terms of what has been said not to its abolition but to its establishment and expansion. In fact, private property is grounded not in human capriciousness but in human nature. Certainly the government has a calling in this respect; in connection with the acquisition, administration, and use of property, the government needs to frame regulations that reduce and restrain related sins. But in general the government has the calling not to abolish private property but to protect it. For private property is not a right that the state has bestowed, but an inalienable right belonging to the person himself. Every person has the right to acquire assets along the route of God's commandment, according to the law that he ordained for that. That is his right, and simultaneously his duty. For a person is distinguished from an animal. An animal seizes what it can to provide for its needs. At night the animal leaves the forest, the young lions roaring for their prey as they seek their food from God's hand; as the sun rises, they return and lie down in their dens [Ps. 104:20–22].

But at that point man goes out to his work and labors until evening. His works are not works of darkness and of predation but works of the light and honest labor. He does not steal and rob, but he works in order to eat and to live; it is his honor and privilege to live from the work of his hands, to provide for his manifold needs by means of what he has produced through honest labor and to which he has acquired a moral right. This right of individual property is still acknowledged even by socialism, insofar as it wants to distinguish in the society of the future between the means of production and the means of consumption and wants wages to be paid according to each person's merit.

Socialism errs, however, in that here as well it loses sight of the rich diversity of society, holding to the abstract theory that a communal standard exists for all labor, according to which such labor in its diverging forms would be able to be justly rewarded by the community. No person and no state can do that. With the distribution of goods, just as with the gifts of emotional and physical strength, notwithstanding the corruption that has intruded here as well, there is a divine ordinance to be respected that must be obediently acknowledged by everybody, one that can be altered or improved by nobody. In this dispensation, things do not proceed, or do not proceed exclusively or in the first place, according to merit, but according to grace. All of society lives from that grace; anyone who wants to ban that grace and replace it at every point with merit, is merely inviting the rule of the worst injustice.

But, no matter how much private property must be acknowledged and protected, the law of God ought to be proclaimed against the terrible sins that abuse private property, a law which also ties that property to moral rules. Here the government has a modest and limited task. The most important is that in their conscience each person and every family must realize that they are bound to the divine commandment in their pursuit of private property. That command calls us to work in the sweat of our brow, for one who does not work will not eat [2 Thess. 3:10]; but it also obligates us to such acquisition, administration, and enjoyment of all property as is consistent with love toward God and neighbor. The sixth commandment of the moral law finds its principle, its limit, and its purpose in love. Every investigation of society, of the relationships in which it consists, and of the goods that it acquires, possesses, and enjoys, leads back to the moral foundations on which society rests. And of these moral foundations, marriage and family constitute the fixed, unshakable cornerstone.

The Family Will Not Disintegrate, but Marriage and Family Will Continue to Exist until God Achieves His Intention with Them

All of the phenomena we have discussed prove that the family, despite being despised and opposed, is far from being registered as dead. Its forms may change, but its essence abides. It is an institution of God, maintained after the entrance of sin not by the will of man but by God's power. And it will continue to be preserved, as long as the divine purpose with the human race has not yet been attained.

That purpose is familiar to Christians from Scripture. For Christians, the future is portrayed entirely differently than for those without faith in any revelation. For apart from revelation, the origin, essence, purpose, and destiny of the human race are entirely unknown to us. Because without this knowledge we cannot live and cannot die, cannot think and cannot labor, the Christian faith is replaced by arbitrary guesses and the Christian hope by vain expectations. People then dream of a future state that will arise automatically through evolution, in which everyone will live happily and contentedly. But in this case it's like a hungry man dreaming that he is eating, but when he awakens, his soul is empty; or like a thirsty man dreaming that he is drinking, but when he awakens, he is still parched and his soul is thirsty.

Christians know about other and better things. They do not look back to the past with homesickness, for even then not everything that glittered was golden. They do not surrender their hearts to the present, for their eyes see the suffering that belongs inseparably to the present time. And they do not fantasize about a perfect society, because in this dispensation sin will continue to hold sway and will constantly corrupt all that is good. But they are assured that God's purpose with the human race will nevertheless be attained, despite all the conflict involved. Humanity and the world exist, after all, for the sake of the church, and the church exists for the sake of Christ's will, and Christ belongs to God. In the city of God the creation reaches its final goal. Into that city all the treasures will be brought together that have been acquired by humanity in the course of time through fearsome conflict; all the glory of the nations is gathered there; and in the spiritual association of Christ with his church, marriage will also reach its end.

Marriage was instituted so that the glory of the King would come to light in the multitude of his subjects. Once it has attained this goal, marriage itself will pass away. The shadow will make way for the substance, the symbol for the reality. The history of the human race began with a wedding; it also ends with a wedding, the wedding of Christ and his church, of the heavenly Lord with his earthly bride.

ABOUT THE CONTRIBUTORS

James Eglinton (PhD, University of Edinburgh) is senior researcher at the Theological University of the Reformed Churches (Liberated), Kampen, the Netherlands. After completing degrees in law (University of Aberdeen) and theology (University of Glasgow), he earned a doctorate in systematic theology at the University of Edinburgh under the supervision of Professor David Fergusson. Following this, he spent two years as a postdoctoral fellow in Kampen, where his work concerned the relationship of Reformed theology in Scotland and the Netherlands. Upon the completion of his postdoctoral period, he was appointed to his current post. From 2007 to 2010, he served as ministerial assistant at St. Columba's Free Church in Edinburgh, Scotland. He is the author of *Trinity and Organism: Towards a New Reading of Herman Bavinck's Organic Motif* (T&T Clark, 2012) and he is married to Eilidh and has a young son, Seumas.

Stephen J. Grabill (PhD, Calvin Theological Seminary) is director of programs and international at the Acton Institute. He is also a senior research scholar in theology, and an adjunct professor of theological ethics at Grand Rapids Theological Seminary. He is the general editor of the *NIV Stewardship Study Bible*, author or editor of eight books, editor emeritus of the *Journal of Markets & Morality*, general editor of Abraham Kuyper's three-volume *Common*

Grace translation project, and coeditor (with Jordan J. Ballor) of a new academic series *Sources in Early Modern Ethics, Economics, and Law* published by Christian's Library Press. He is also responsible for providing direction and oversight to Acton's new evangelical audience extension efforts through strategic network building, curriculum creation, and intellectual outreach. He is married to Rebecca and is blessed with four children who are Nicholas, Sebastian, Magdalene, and Penelope.

Nelson D. Kloosterman (ThD, Theological University of the Reformed Churches (Liberated), Kampen, the Netherlands) serves as ethics consultant for Worldview Resources International (St. John, Indiana, USA), a Christian service organization that provides resources for applying a Christian worldview to living in a global culture. His earned degrees include a bachelor of divinity (Calvin Theological Seminary) and a doctor of theology. For more than twenty-five years he taught courses in ethics, New Testament, and preaching on the seminary level. He has translated and published several books, including *The Ten Commandments: Manual for the Christian Life* and *Responsible Conduct: Principles of Christian Ethics* both by J. Douma, *Preaching and the History of Salvation* by C. Trimp, and *Saved by Grace: The Holy Spirit's Work in Calling and Regeneration* by Herman Bavinck. His current Dutch-English translation projects include a twenty-three-volume commentary, *Opening the Scriptures*, and cotranslating and editing *Common Grace* and *Pro Rege*, the latter two by Abraham Kuyper.

SCRIPTURE INDEX

Old Testament

Genesis

1	66
1:27	3, 34, 65n3
12:14	33
16	33
16:2	33
16:6	33
18:12	31
2	66
2:18	111
2:18–24	34
2:24	35
20:12	31
24:3	31
24:8	33
24:15–16	33
24:20	76
27:29	33
27:37	33
28:1	76
29:9	33
29:10	33
29:14	31
29:24	33
29:29	33
3	9
3:12	16
30:4	33
30:9	33
34:11	76
38:6	76
38:24	35
4:8	16
4:23–24	16
43:29	31
49:3	33
49:8	33

Exodus

2:16	33 (2x)
12:26	34
15:20–21	33
19:6	30
20:2	34
20:5–6	32
20:12	34
20:14	35
20:17	31, 33
21:15	34
22:19	35
28:42	35

Leviticus

9:3	34n1
15:18	35
18:18	31
18:19	35
18:22–23	35
19:3	34
19:11–17	30
19:18	30
19:29	35
20:6	36

20:9	34	**1 Samuel**		**Isaiah**	
20:10	35	1	33	1:21	36
20:13	35	2:19	33	5	36
20:18	35	8:13	33	33:22	31
		9:11	33	45:18	2
Numbers		18:6–7	33	49:15	3
14:33	36			51:1	36
30	31	**2 Samuel**		53:11	119
		13:8	33	61:10	36
Deuteronomy		20:16	33	62:5	36
4:9	34			63:16	36
17:19–20	31	**1 Kings**		64:8	36
21:15	31	12	31	66:13	3
21:15–17	33				
21:18–19	31	**Psalms**		**Jeremiah**	
22:22	35	27:10	3	2:21	36
23:13–14	35	73:27	36	2:32	36
23:17–18	35	103:13	3	3:1	36
23:21–23	42	104:20–22	158	51:1	36n2
24:1	31	127:3	33		
32:4	36	139:13–16	90	**Ezekiel**	
32:6	36			16	36
32:18	36	**Proverbs**		16:32	36
33:4	36n2	2:17	34	16:38–41	35
33:18	36n2	12:4	35	16:8	34
		18:22	35	18:6	35
Judges		19:14	35	22:10	35
9:1–2	31	31:10–28	96	23:43–49	35
14:1	33	31:10–31	33, 34, 35	**Hosea**	
14:1–5	31	31:29–30	34	1–3	35, 36
16:27	33			2:18	34
Ruth		**Ecclesiastes**		**Malachi**	
2:5–6	33	2:21	119	2:14	34

Scripture Index

New Testament

Matthew

5:17–20	41
5:27–28	41
5:32	42
8:14	44
10:37	42
15:4–6	43
15:19	51
17:14–20	43
18:3	43, 8
18:5	43
19:4–6	42
19:5	35
19:6	7
19:8	7
19:9	42
19:12	41, 71
19:13–15	43
21:16	43
22:30	41
22:39	30
24:19	41

Mark

3:32–35	39
7:10–12	43
10:8	35

Luke

1:38	38
2:49	40
2:52	39
7:11–15	43
7:36–50	40
8:41–56	43
11:27–28	37

John

2:4	40
4:27	40
4:34	40
4:46–54	43
8:11	40
19:26–27	40

Acts

1:14	49
2:39	46
4:20	49n4 (2x)
5:14	49
12:12	49 (2x)
17:4	49, 49n4
17:12	49

Romans

1:26–32	47
5:12	9
16	49
16:1	49
16:3	49
16:6–15	49

1 Corinthians

5:10	45
6:16	35, 46
7:1–9	53
7:1–17	44
7:2	46
7:11	47
7:12–14	47
7:14	45, 46
7:15	47
7:22	49
7:39	45
9:5	44
10:27	45
11:3–9	82
11:5	49
11:7	3
11:7–9	44
11:8–9	7
14:34	9, 49
15:22	9
16:19	49

2 Corinthians

6:14	45
9:5	44n1

Galatians

3:28	45

Ephesians

4:24	70
5:22–23	82
5:22–33	46
5:25–30	81
5:26–27	40
5:31	35, 46 (2x)
5:32	44
5:33	46
6:1	46
6:1–3	46
6:4	46

Colossians

3:1	70
3:18	82, 85
3:18–19	46
3:19	81
3:20–21	46
4:15	49

2 Thessalonians

3:10	159

1 Timothy

2:12	49
2:12–14	9, 44
2:12–15	82
2:15	46, 96
3:2	46, 46n2
3:11	49
3:12	46
3:22	46n2 (2x)
4:3–5	44
4:4	88
5:3–16	49
6:9	129

Titus

1:6	46
2:5	82

Hebrews

12:6	3
13:4	44

James

1:17	8, 124

1 Peter

2:9	46
3:1	49, 83
3:1–7	46
3:7	46, 68, 81 (2x)

Made in the USA
Middletown, DE
24 December 2023